Queen
of
Blackpool

Pat Mancini

Polperro Heritage Press

ISBN 09553648 9 2
978-09553648-9-1

Cover design by Simon Hammond

Published by
Polperro Heritage Press
Clifton-upon-Teme
Worcestershire WR6 6EN
United Kingdom
polperro.press@virgin.net

Printed by
Orphans Press Ltd
Leominster
Herefordshire
HR6 0LD
United Kingdom

Foreword

It's a great privilege to write the foreword to my life-long friend Pat Mancini's autobiography. A more loving, caring person it would be difficult to find than the author of this book.

Her work for charities in and around Blackpool is legendary and has deservingly earned her the prestigious trip to Buckingham Palace to be presented with an MBE by His Royal Highness, the Prince of Wales.

There is no more gracious and humorous hotel owning resident in Blackpool. The Queens Hotel in South Promenade is the favourite venue for all of us in show business. Pat is always a generous hostess. So get a glass of your favourite tipple, put your feet up and take your time reading her book. She has had an amazing life and her stories will keep you interested. It's the way she tells 'em!

She's a cracker.

Frank Carson
November 2008

For Dean and Pamela, my mother Vivian and Rudi

Acknowledgements

I am especially grateful to Stafford Hildred who both encouraged me and helped me write my story.

To all my family and friends: my dearest granddaughters, Adele and Gemma; my sister Sharron and her husband Raymond; my brother Paul and his wife Doreen, and my life-long friends Eric and Sylvia Brown. Special thanks to my general manager Joe Pisacane and his wife Alice, my head receptionist, for their loyal and devoted service for 23 years. My dear friend Mark Simpson who has been by my side for 15 years, Bobby Ball and his wife Yvonne, and Garry Bushell. My friends Peter Anthony and Paul Lomax, Johnny Casson, Roy 'Chubby' Brown and his wife Helen; Anne-Marie and Eric Slack, Mick and Wendy Miller, Tony Joe and Helen; Joe Longthorne and his partner Jamie, also Fr Geoffrey Bottoms from the Sacred Heart church in Blackpool for his support and guidance to Joe, Jamie and myself through some difficult times. My sincere thanks to everyone who has helped and supported me since I lost my dear Rudi ten years ago.

A special word of gratitude to Frank Carson for writing the foreword to this book. And, finally, very special thanks to Jeremy Beadle who gave me so much encouragement to write this book and yet sadly never lived to see it in print. I do miss you Jeremy.

Contents

Introduction

The happiest day of my life came on my 25th wedding anniversary to my beloved husband Rudi. We celebrated with a trip to Paris, to stay at the swanky Ritz Hotel. As we stepped out of the limo that had brought us from the airport Rudi turned to me with his typical shy smile and said, 'How the bleedin' hell did we get here?'

We both laughed and then kissed tenderly. He didn't need to say any more. With that wonderful familiarity that comes from true love he had neatly summed up my own feelings of sheer bliss. We both knew what a difficult and rocky road we'd had to travel to finally triumph over some pretty horrendous adversities and share just about as blissful a relationship that a man and a woman can have.

From the back streets of Manchester we had travelled a journey full of heartache and tragedy to eventually carve out our little piece of paradise. To be totally honest the Queens Hotel, Blackpool is not exactly little. It's the largest privately owned hotel in the most vibrant seaside resort in Britain. But to Rudi and myself, the proud owners of that wonderful old star of the seafront, the Queens is much more than just a hotel. It's a symbol of a lifetime of our true love and of a lifetime of hard work.

Sadly, Rudi is no longer alive to share my life at the Queens, but I still own and run the place. That brief break at the Ritz was to be one of our last memories as well as one of the happiest. Typically our life was not incident free, even in the swishest of hotels. Soon after we arrived they came up and said, 'You'll have to move rooms because there's a water leak in yours.' We were a bit put out until we saw where they moved us. It was into the Coco Chanel Suite, one of the Ritz's finest. It was where the legendary fashion designer spent the War and it was just fine for Rudi and myself for a few days.

Since my husband died ten years ago I have thrown myself into charity work to help to fill the aching gap in my world. Sometimes for a short time it almost works, but while I have breath left in my body I would like to tell you the story of my life.

It begins in very humble beginnings in Manchester where I first met Rudi. We were both married to other people when we fell in love and the pain and anguish began. We hurt a lot of people but we were simply overwhelmed by our emotions. We tried hard to resist our feelings for each other but in the end they were just too powerful. To this day I feel guilt about walking out on my young son and daughter and my husband, but after reading this book I hope you'll at least understand my actions.

Fortunately there have been lots of highs as well as lows along the way. I hope you enjoy the ride!

1

Childhood

I was born on 11 April in 1939 in a small, working class suburb of Manchester called Bradford. I had a wonderful loving mother and a large caring family, but I never knew my father. He went away to fight in the Second World War the year I was born, and he was killed in 1944, just as he was supposed to be coming home on leave for the first time. He was travelling back from Malta and the fighting was so bad in Italy the ship was diverted there. He was sent to Monte Cassino and within a fortnight he was killed in action. He was just 24 years old. So he never did come home. People felt sorry for me but because I never knew him, I never missed him. To me it feels as if I never had a father.

The family first lived in a very crowded two up and two down, terraced house with my grandma, who I always called 'Ninny' and my granddad. They had eight children so I had loads of aunties and uncles around in our very close-knit family and I always remember the atmosphere in the house as being very happy and full of love. By modern standards I suppose we were positively poverty stricken but we always had enough to eat and everyone else had their toilet in their back yards so I never felt remotely deprived. Ninny and my granddad gave birth to six boys, my father Richard who was the oldest, and his brothers Terence, Lawrence, Henry, Edward and Jim, and two girls, Vera and Helen.

My early world was a collection of streets full of almost identical small terraced houses. They have all long gone now as the whole area has long since been redeveloped out of recognition. All my relations lived nearby and when I was very small we enjoyed a little more space after my mother rented another house, also in John Street, Bradford. It was just across the road. Ninny's house was number 11 while my mother rented number 20. I'm not sure when she got it but I can't remember sleeping in Ninny's house. Me and my mother slept in the same bed in one bedroom and my aunts Vera and Helen came over and slept in the other bedroom. Before then I simply don't know how they had ever managed in a two up and two down with girls and lads living in the same place but somehow they did it. It was real life Coronation Street exactly. Those backyards were not big but we also had chickens there in the air raid shelter. I used to have to go and feed them before I went to school. They would try to run after me and I would shoo them back in. I became really fond of them. They were like pets they were so friendly but then at Christmas we used to kill them and eat them.

After the War we used to play in the shelters. Some of them had bunk beds in. We used to have some great times. Everything seemed very stable throughout my childhood. In those days everyone had a father and mother who were just about always still together in a family unit. That's what was so different when I was growing up. I felt as if I was part of a huge extended family as the neighbours were our friends and relations.

I remember we had some wonderful street parties for the end of the War. I remember my uncle Henry coming home. He was in the RAF and in my mind's eye I can see him now, a great big man looking so smart in his blue uniform. My grandmother cried when he came home and I couldn't understand why. Now I think maybe she was sad because my dad, her eldest son, was not coming home. But there wasn't just one celebration after the War had been won. There was a party every time someone came home. All the neighbours would make sandwiches and there was jelly and custard and biscuits and cakes and you'd all have to bring a cup and saucer. We'd put bunting up and it was great.

Everybody knew everybody in those days. No-one locked their door when I was a kid. We used to be in and out of neighbours' houses all the time. My mum was often sending me for a cup of sugar or some tea. I don't think they even locked the doors at night. From being quite tiny I was sent to the shop. I remember Ninny who often had a bad stomach always wanted Indian Brandy and composition. In those days you could get things on tick if you were a bit short until the end of the week. Once the shopkeeper was fed up of someone owing him money for a little too long and he put a note in the window naming the guilty person. That night he had a brick put through his window. I don't think he tried that particular credit control tactic any more. That was your community - all around you. You didn't need community centres. The church, the pub on the corner and the street: they were our community centres. Just about everything happened in the street. We made our own entertainment. The street seemed to almost have a personality of its own. You could tell the time by the sounds of the street. You knew the sounds of the morning when everyone was rushing to school or to work. Even if you were inside the house you knew when Sunday was because everything was quiet, until the ice-cream man came round. Of course there were only a few cars around in those days so sounds of street life were much easier to distinguish. But I can remember lying ill in bed, on one of the few occasions I was off school poorly and listening to the noises outside and I could always tell what time of day it was. You could hear the sound of skipping ropes on the concrete after school and you felt part of it all.

One of my very first memories is of being taken to school by a neighbour called Mrs Rodgers who lived across the road. This was very different because normally Ninny took me. I was only five years old, but I knew that there was something going on. I know now that the news had come through that my dad had been killed. But I didn't know then. Even when I came home nobody told me what had happened. In those days children were kept in the dark, in our house at any rate. Today no doubt the social services would send counsellors round to tell you gently that your daddy is going to heaven but in those days you were just left to work it out for yourself. I knew something was wrong but I didn't know what. Later of course it became clear that my father was dead. It didn't have the impact some people seem to expect because the honest truth was that I had never known him so I never missed him.

My earliest memories are of the details of our life. Before school every morning I had to go to the shop for my grandmother and buy a quarter of corned beef or a bit of liver or whatever she wanted. I used to get up about eight o'clock because it was about a quarter of an hour away on foot, which was the only method of travel open to me at the time. I always used to pinch a slice of corned beef and eat it cold and grab a sausage and eat it raw. That was one of my favourites, raw sausage.

Usually I was healthy but one day in school I was shivering and feeling sickly. I was hot at the same time so I must have had a cold coming on. In those days all they did was send you home to bed. There was a massive road to cross on the way home, but nobody ever seemed too concerned of the dangers of things like that. I can't recall anyone having any fear about children roaming around unaccompanied. I was so cold and it had been snowing and I got to the road and felt so poorly I must have looked a pathetic sight. But I remember as I was waiting to cross the road this boxy little car went past and inside was a woman wearing a beautiful fur coat. And I looked at her with my first flash of real envy and I thought, 'She is warm and snug in that lovely coat in that car and I am standing outside in the snow freezing. I hope I am never this cold again'. It sounds as if I'm trying to put adult thoughts into a child's mind but I swear I thought to myself, 'One day I'm going to have a car and a warm fur coat to keep out the cold'. I've carried the image of that woman in my mind ever since. Now I've got two mink coats and a fox, not that you can wear them to go out without somebody disapproving. I've got a Rolls Royce and a Jaguar in the garage as well. But I often think back to that moment of envy. I was so cold that day my teeth were chattering and when I eventually got home Ninny gave me a hot drink and put me to bed as always. In a couple of days I was back at school. Ninny's own health was not so good. She was a very large lady and she was a diabetic, who had to inject herself with insulin in the morning. If ever I smell metholated spirits, which she used to sterilise the injection, it takes me straight back to my early childhood. She used to take me into town and the treat was to queue up in Littlewoods and have a cup of tea and a cake. She always bought enough cakes to take some home. They were the best cakes. I was always conscious of other kids staring at Ninny, maybe because she was so big. All my father's side of the family were quite dark. My uncle Laurence used to tease me by calling me 'Big Nose'. It gave me quite an inferiority complex for a while but Ninny told me I hadn't got a big nose at all. I just had my father's nose, that's all. I was pleased with that.

The Whit Walks were one of the great traditions when I was growing up in Manchester. Our school, St Bridget's in Bradford, had its own band and in the grand parade we all marched along proudly behind it. All the church banners were flying and we all met in Albert Square. It was great fun. We all had to give our measurements to C&A to get your uniform for the big occasion. We paid so much a week and you couldn't wait to get it home to show your mum what you looked like in your uniform. We never had school uniforms, it was only if you went to high school that you got one. That was why we thought they were posh because while they looked very smart we just wore our ordinary clothes to go to school. After the Whit Walk you could wear your dress for school and we felt much smarter then. I've never understood why people criticise school uniforms. When I was a kid we always wanted to look smart and we'd have loved a proper school uniform. We loved to have our 'matching' clothes for Whit Week. It was the one time of the year when you had a load of clothes and everything was new. We had new underwear, socks, liberty bodices, cotton underskirt, everything. It felt fabulous. We had loads of layers of clothes because layers keep you warm. That's an old truth that has come back today.

Looking back, I had a wonderful upbringing. My best friend at school was a girl called Veronica Field. She lived in the same street as me and she had a father who used to give her a belt. She showed me the marks on her body where he had hit her. I can remember thinking at the time, 'I'm glad I haven't got a dad if that's what they do to you'. I was chastised and I was even taken to the police station once to frighten me. Being in trouble in those days was not what it is today. I remember one of the worst things we did was accidentally breaking the mantle of a gas lamp. We were brought up very strictly. My mum never ever told me she loved me. We weren't an openly emotional family but I always knew she loved me and I loved her. I always did. This openly emotional kissing business that is so common nowadays is very hard for me. Throwing your arms round a complete stranger doesn't rest well with me at all. Times have changed so much. In one way I think it is wonderful the way people are more able to express their feelings for each other today but the respect that we had for older people has gone and that is not so good. Grown ups were given respect whether they were neighbours, doctors, teachers or just aunties and uncles. We never gave back chat and it was always Mrs So and So or Mr This. We never ever disrespected a neighbour. Not that we were goodie-goodies. We larked about knocking on the doors and running away. That was just about the naughtiest thing we ever did, though one night after the bunting for a party had been put up we pulled some of it down.

St Bridget's was a Roman Catholic school. It was junior and senior and the girls school was always separate from the boys. Girls never mixed with boys apart from at Benediction. We used to have to go to Mass every Thursday for Benediction and that's the only time we saw the opposite sex. One lad I got to know quite well in those days was Frank Pearson who always sang in church with a beautiful high voice. Frank went on to become much better known in Manchester and the north as Frank 'Foo

Foo' Lamar but that is another story that he has already told himself. I was always very happy at school. I had a great time. I only played truant once in my life from school. We just wanted to go out. We had a note to go to the dental clinic. My mate was going to the clinic with warts and scabs and the sorts of things you used to get in those days. I pretended I had been up all night with toothache and I had to go to the dentist. When I got there he examined me and insisted on taking a tooth out! I never tried that trick again.

When it came to going out with boys, I was a very late developer. We played with lads on the street all our youth from being young kids. I suppose with kids from the neighbouring streets we were a gang. We played hide and seek, rally-vo together. We played skipping games where the lads used to turn the ropes for us but there was no sexual side to it at all. There was rivalry with other streets: our street's better than yours, but it was friendly not nasty or violent. I remember there was some chasing after each other but I can't remember any fighting, which seems incredible when you think what kids of today get up to.

The only violence I ever saw in my upbringing in the local community was two fellows coming out of a pub and putting their fists up and having a fight. There were ordinary, everyday things like women neighbours rowing with their husbands when they came home from the pub late. We used to sit on the steps late, because the bugs were coming out, as they used to say. Mrs Blair next door used to tell us stories and we were really fascinated. One night a man called Mr Fenton, who had a big, big family, came home drunk and he was banging on the door demanding to be let in. His wife opened the upstairs window and threw the contents of the pee bucket all over him. That was headline news up and down the street.

It was a much more stable society in those days. Everyone had a mum and dad and brothers and sisters had the same mum and dad. People stayed in their houses for years. They couldn't afford to move and the jobs were all there locally.

The houses might not have much in the way of mod cons but they were full of love. It all went wrong, in my view, when the planners knocked all these cosy little homes down and picked families up and put them in high rise flats. Hiding them all in boxes was the biggest mistake of all because those communities were living, breathing groups of people who knew each other and helped each other out through thick and thin. That's all gone now.

When I was growing up there was a reassuring predictability about life. If you died somebody laid you out. If someone was getting married we all got together and took the meat to the corner shop to cut it on the bacon slicer and made a buffet for them. We all made cakes and did everything to make it a great day. The neighbours were all involved. Everyone would come out to wave you off when you got married. You knew everybody's business because they had nothing to hide. Nobody had any money, people wore clogs a lot and pinnys to protect their clothes. Those days were just so different. There were no social workers to tell you how to behave, no busy-bodies to tell you how to run your life, and hardly any benefits if you did hit trouble. One of my friends was Rhona Webb and her parents kept the corner shop. I remember her parents telling me that the next day they were to start selling the first sliced loaves of bread. This was quite an event in John Street and Ninny and I went up to get the very first one. Mrs Webb laughed when she saw me and said, 'I thought you'd be here early with your Nan.'

I think I was about eight years old when I came running back home with the first sliced loaf in our street. That is one of my happiest memories - even if one of the unhappiest was just around the corner. The most frightening experience of my young life came when I was nine years old and I was sent on holiday to Belgium. It was supposed to be a treat but to me it was a terrifying nightmare. My mum got a letter from the local authorities saying that children who had lost their fathers in the War were to receive a free holiday, courtesy of some of the people on the continent who had helped us in the battle against the Germans. Two children out of every school were chosen and I was selected to go and stay with a family in Brussels - for a month! Everyone seemed very excited about this great adventure but I was scared stiff. Suddenly I was packing all my dresses and getting my hat and coat and I was sent off with other children from Manchester on the train to London. We all queued up at London Road Station, as it was known in those days, and off we went. I was with a girl called Pat Carroll from our school and we soon made friends with the others on the way down. We stayed overnight in London and I was suffering from the worst toothache I've had in my life. I was in agony. It was awful. I cried all night long. There was nobody to turn to and I felt so helpless and alone. Next day we were put on a boat and I felt more and more worried. As the boat journey went on I just kept thinking, 'How is my mum going to find me now?' I had never even been to London before, let alone abroad.

Eventually we got off the boat and there were people there to meet us. I was picked up by car and taken to an address, which I'm sure was 42 Rue Paul Lauters. It was a big, imposing town house with railings outside and a basement down below. On the door it had a speaker where you pressed a button to talk to the people inside. They're common nowadays but in the late 1940s they were practically unheard of. It was a massive family house occupied by the Francert family and every member was lined up to meet little me. All these people were so elegant and well-dressed and the house seemed like a palace. It had towering high ceilings and chandeliers hanging down. They were dead posh and I was mesmerised by it all. I just kept thinking, 'My mother will never find me now'. I'm sure the family all thought they were doing me a favour but they had no idea how bad I felt about leaving home. I was very unhappy. I didn't know anybody. Pat Carroll had gone off to another family so I was just there on my own. It was a real ordeal. At meal times we all sat round this enormous table. I was confronted by all this cutlery and a row of crystal glasses going up in height. The food was another problem. I ate some strange stuff but I drew the line at snails. They regarded them as a delicacy but I managed to say *non* to snails. They allowed me to have a small drink of wine. Apparently that's normal on the continent and I suppose they were celebrating my arrival but I knew I was really too young to drink wine. Then they showed me my bedroom … in the basement. It was a lovely room and beautifully furnished but there were bars on the window, which made me feel like a prisoner. That frightened me a little but my hosts were very nice and kind to me. Unfortunately I was so upset by everything that the first night I wet the bed. I had never done that at home since I was a little kid and I did it for quite a few nights. They did shout at me for that.

I was just so unhappy and so unbearably lonely there. I was convinced I would never see my mum and my happy home ever again. To be fair, the Belgian family did try to cheer me up. I remember being taken out to see a big lion at the zoo one day. But some of the other kids in the street were not so friendly. When I used to go to the front gate to see these children playing they taunted me by pointing and shouting, 'English, English!' I used to run back in terrified. I never played with any other kids in the street. I was just too frightened of them. It was a really awful time. And a month is a long time when you're ten years old. These days I am sure a child would not be treated like this, but when I was growing up children were expected to keep quiet and do as they were told. Eventually my time in Brussels came to an end and I was delighted to start the journey home. Still desperately worried that my mother would not know where to find me I bought some strange new three-cornered chocolate on the boat. I had discovered Toblerone. Of course my mother was waiting when I got off the train at London Road Station and I was very, very relieved. A month is a long time when you're missing your mum.

Secondary school was still St Bridget's, as I failed my 11 plus and stayed at the secondary part of the same school. Life became different then as we started to grow up. I loved sport and we used to play rounders and netball and swimming. We never won anything in our school ever but we were quite good at swimming. There were four of us who really loved it. The swimming teacher got us in a competition between different schools. Amazingly we got to the finals. It was such a big thing. Nobody ever heard of St Bridget's in Bradford doing anything. It was always posh colleges and other well known schools doing well. On the morning of the big finals we had to meet our swimming teacher on Ashton New Road near the new Royal picture house that had opened, at 10 oclock on a Saturday morning. There were four girls in the team for the relay race but one girl didn't turn up. We waited and waited for ages until it was too late and we had to go. We had a reserve of course. We got on the bus and went to the big pool down at Rusholme. We got there and the first girl went in and did well and I swam and we were winning by half a length. All our friends were screaming and shouting because this was unprecedented. St Bridget's never came anywhere at anything in those days. The opposition girls all seemed to be bigger and stronger than us, I had never seen girls like them, but we were winning by half a length. It was amazing. Everyone was going mad. But the reserve had to be put in and she swam under the rope and out of her lane and we were disqualified into last place. It was awful. We definitely would have won. The girl who didn't turn up was called Kathleen O'Brien. She just overslept. Jesus, when she got to school next day she took some stick from the head teacher for letting us down, letting herself down, letting the school down.

Not so many years ago she walked into the Queens Hotel and as soon as I saw her I recognised her. I said, 'You're Kathleen O'Brien'. I knew her right away. She was one of my best friends at school. Her oversleeping was just one of those things I suppose but it was a terrible disappointment at the time. The reason we were so desperate to win was that we all wanted to take the cup round the lads' school next door just to show them. They often won medals and cups with football and their games but we never won everything and our one big chance was taken away from us. It never happened. It was not just swimming I loved at school; I did netball, rounders and other sports and everyone seemed to join in. It's not like today when you see kids who are just too fat to join in. We had been through the War and nobody was fat. There was just one girl in the class who was slightly plump but not by today's standards. She was called Pat Barratt and she had rosy cheeks and she was just solidly built and she wasn't fat at all.

There were no great big bloated wobbly arses like you see on so many of the girls, and boys sometimes, of today. No one got fat because we were all playing all the time. We either played sports at school or we played out at night after school. We were never still. There was no TV to watch, no play stations to be glued to all night. We had to make our own entertainment and that was what we did. All the time. We played for hours with skipping ropes, we did handstands on the wall. We were the best exercised kids in the world. And we had good food, my mum always made sure of that. We all went to school dinners and I got mine cheaper because my dad had got killed in the War. Some got free dinners, there were some very poor families around in those days. But we just loved playing out. We roamed all over and our mothers couldn't get us in because we had such a good time playing in the street. It was always one more handstand, one more hopscotch, one more game of whatever it was that we were playing. I suppose by today's standards we were hard up but I never felt it. I never felt I missed out on anything. It was a very innocent upbringing when you compare our lives with the kids of today.

I feel so sorry for the current generation of kids. They don't seem to have time to enjoy a proper childhood. Young girls still at primary school come in to my hotel with make-up on. We used to dress up. We loved it, but we were never allowed to put make-up on. In my back yard we used to dress up as the May Queens, getting old curtains or whatever we could lay our hands on. Then we would go round from house to house hoping to get a penny or two and we would share it out equally between us afterwards.

My mother took the curtain down for me to wear. They were taffeta and very thin in a lilac colour that I can never forget. We were going roller skating to Birch Park in Rusholme as we used to do on a Saturday afternoon. We cut them up and made this little skating outfit with a short skirt and top. Girls who came from families with money who went there had proper smart skating outfits, so for once we thought we could match up to them. Three or four of us went and we thought we looked really good, until we started skating. The material was so thin and rotted that as soon as we started moving it just fell apart all around us and we were left standing in our knickers. It just disintegrated. It was so embarrassing. That was life back then. In those days you made your own fun. My mother always worked terribly hard. She kept working until she died at 83. I think it was what helped to keep her going, she had to be doing something. I never knew her not work.

When I was about 13 I wanted to go and play netball. I was in the netball team but I couldn't go and play because I had all these jobs to do for my mum before she came home from work. Every night I had to make the fire, brush up, put paper on the table and set the table for tea. So I stayed off dinners and saved my threepence dinner money to give to another girl to pay her to go home and do my jobs (even in those days I knew how to get my own staff).

These days it would be considered too dangerous to let kids light a fire. Even then I once had a terrible accident when I let a cinder fall out and set fire to a pouffe in the lounge. It's a good job I was still there to put it out otherwise the whole house would probably have burned down. I got into trouble for that. Before modern electricity was installed we used accumulators, which were just batteries with acid in. We used to have to go to the shop to pick up accumulators full of acid. It was incredibly dangerous but it was just one of our jobs and no-one batted an eyelid. These days Health and Safety would blow a fuse.

But I think that kids in those days were brought up to be more sensible. We were shown how to do things much more than children are today. I learned how to bake and cook because my mother showed me how and taught me from a very young age. We did it together. She showed me how to clean the house properly. How many kids today have that experience? It sticks with you. I used to go for coal or coke in the depths of a freezing winter with a big barrow with big iron wheels on, but in those days you did as you were told. I wasn't being abused, I was just doing my job. It was a real chore and I hated it but they weren't being cruel to us, everybody did it.

We certainly learned about life early on. The pawn shop was somewhere my mother never wanted to go but other families were not so fortunate. One girl who is still my best friend today had a mother who was always having to visit the pawn shop. Her mum was an alcoholic and she used to take her husband's shirt down to the pawn shop to get money and then desperately struggle to get it out of pawn before he wanted to go out in it on a Saturday.

In those days you took a bundle of clothes down to get money and my friend's mum's ambition was to get the whole bundle out. Her dream was to get to the front of the queue and announce in front of everyone that she wanted everything out and she had the money to pay for it. It would only have cost her a few pennies but that seemed like a fortune to her because any spare money she ever had she bought booze with. She finally managed it and she was absolutely delighted and made sure everyone knew that while they might have been poor they were out of debt at last.

Sundays were great when I was a kid. The main thing in our house was baking for the week ahead. There would be a great big table full of everything you could think of, mince pies, apple pies, whimberry pies, and all the other kinds of pies. My mum was a wonderful cook. And later when all the work was done we would get the dominoes out and play with my granddad. He never drank or even went out very much. My life was just very, very family orientated. My mother never smoked and she hated the smell. One of the strongest were Pasha cigarettes and my mother went mad if she smelt it. 'Who's smoking Pasha?' she would shout angrily if she smelt so much as a whiff.

The cinema was a great thing in those days. I used to love to go to the cinema. We would stand up in the queues for hours to get in and we never minded the wait. We used to go to the Mosley, the Don, and the New Royal on Ashton New Road. On Sundays we would go to the New Royal in the afternoon and down to the Don at night. We would stand patiently in the queue until eventually two people would be allowed in if two people came out. We went in when it was our turn without thinking if the film had started or not. We always seemed to go in the cinema halfway through the film so we would watch the end before the beginning. We waited until it was 'where we came in'. As soon as that happened we would get up and walk out. It was as if we were brainwashed to leave at the point. We were grateful just to be let in. All day I would be excited in anticipation and then when our big moment came they would say 'There's room for two at the back, standing' and we would rush in as if we had won first prize in the Lottery.

Films used to whisk you away from the boring, every day grind of life. They were magic. We would come out and the girls would be dancing and the lads would be playing out some cowboy adventure they had just seen. It was a big treat just to be taken to the cinema. The musicals were always my favourites. I loved Doris Day when I was a kid. I used to dream of becoming an actress and singing and dancing like her. She was my heroine, I suppose. When I was younger I used to be taken to the cinema twice a week, once by my Uncle Henry and he said, 'You always know when it's over because the director's name comes up, when that happens it's the start of the film.' I was only a kid. These things stick in my mind. My school career was full of contradictions. I was made milk monitor and I hate milk. I always have. I used to smell it on the tables. My head is still full of memories of childhood. All through school I did some sort of dancing, whether it was tap dancing, Irish dancing, Scottish dancing, all sorts. I was in several different dance troupes and always loved dancing.

At school I loved it when I got a chance to act and I was always in the plays. We did a play for the Festival of Britain and our school put it on at Mosley Street Library Theatre. It was Shakespeare's *A Midsummer Night's Dream*. I was in it and I enjoyed every minute even if I didn't understand it. Nobody knew what they were talking about, we just said the words. We were doing it the next day and going through it over and over again with this teacher I loved called Miss McIlvenny. She was my most favourite teacher of all time and I think she took a little liking to me and was always very encouraging. She taught us for geography and I got on with her so well and wanted to impress her so much that I came first. I astonished myself, it was the first time I had ever come top in anything. I didn't know anything about geography the year before or the year after. It was just that year being taught by Miss McIlvenny was brilliant.

I was 12 and I hadn't the remotest clue what the blinking play meant. I knew we were in the woods and I was playing a workman. My mother sat with me every night in bed for weeks going through all these lines with me. One of my friends, Maureen Lord, who has sadly died now, God rest her soul, only had the one line. She just had to say 'I can roar like a lion'. She had loads of practices and rehearsals.

When it came to the play, Maureen couldn't do it. Her mouth opened and nothing came out. I knew the line. Everyone knew the line. But Maureen Lord simply couldn't bring herself to say the line. She just froze. It must have been nerves or something but she was never quite the same after that. Her lip curled upwards and although it did wear off a little bit after time she never quite went back to normal, how she had looked before. Whether she had a small stroke or what I have no idea and in those days no-one asked those sorts of questions. But we did this play and it went very well. Fancy giving us Shakespeare at a school like ours. We didn't know who he was, where he'd been or what he'd done. Apparently the production was considered to be very successful and then they took us to London to see all the exhibitions. That was the second time I'd been to London. I don't think I was that impressed.

My favourite days out with the school were to Blackpool, or Fleetwood because it wasn't as busy. In Blackpool we always used to stay in a boarding house at 22 Haig Road with Mr and Mrs Waddington. Sheila Waddington used to let me help her clear the tables and I loved it! Our whole family went except for my mother. Laurence, my youngest uncle, would come and so would my aunts Vera and Helen, but not my mother. She never seemed able to take time off from work and she would come over for the occasional day out to see us. My mother was never quite really treated like one of the family, but I was too young to realise it at the time. When we got on the beach our job was to dig in the sand and make a backrest for my Ninny to sit down against. She was too big for a deckchair!

I have so many memories of Blackpool as a kid. Once when I was little I went for an ice cream and my mum told me she would meet me by the steps. When I turned to come back there were lots of steps and I realised I was lost. The beach was really crowded and I just sat waiting and playing until later the beach cleared and my mum could see me.

There was a fish and chip shop on the corner near the boarding house and I remember on one trip I had bought chips and got into terrible trouble for it. My grandfather was outraged to see me eating chips in the street and smacked me on the bottom. He was upset because he thought Mrs Waddington might see me and think I was making out we had not been given enough to eat. It seems amazing now that you had to worry about your landlady's feelings in those days!

They used to put us on the beach for a day and then bring us home again at night-time. I used to love the simple things in life, like going to the park with a bottle of water and a sandwich. That's all we were ever given and we would be in the park all day. I used to love going to Marple and Rosehill on the train from the local railway station at Ashbury. We used to lark about on the coaches and we would stay out all day. It was exciting and so was going to Belle Vue. We used to go on bank holidays or Easter and have a great time. Belle Vue was really swinging in those days. They used to have great big glamorous ballrooms and speedway races. We spent all our time and what money we had on the fairground and the rides just seemed so exciting. But Blackpool was always my favourite. They were magical days out at the seaside.

2

Three's A Crowd

My mum took her time in filling the house with bits of furniture to get it just how she wanted it. By the time I was 12 or 13 she had a table and a few chairs and it was starting to look as if it might be a real home. She was on her own for a long time but after a while she started doing this courting. Not that I knew anything about it at first. I was always out so I did not know what was happening in that part of my mum's life. My mum didn't go out very much. Maybe she would go out with the girls once or twice a month, because Ninny used to keep an eye on her. Whether my grandma felt proprietorial because of her son, my mum's husband, being killed, I don't know. I always remember my mother was very, very introvert. She was always very quiet and would never speak to anyone unless she was directly spoken to. It is just the way she was.

I was 14 when another man came into the house. My mum and I had become very close and it was a shock and a huge change for all of us. She waited a long time before she began another relationship. We never spoke about her feelings but I suppose it was difficult.

She had loved my father very much and she must have been devastated when he was killed. But then she remained living surrounded by my father's family, so there was always a sort of unwritten pressure to preserve her status, even though her husband was dead. I think my grandmother expected my

29

mother to stay on her own and look after me. Before she met the man who later became my stepfather she did meet another man, a very quiet man called Norman. He was a similar character to herself, very shy and self-effacing. He wanted to emigrate to Rhodesia to work on the railways and he asked her to go with him. My mother could not make up her mind whether or not to go. It was an enormous challenge for her and very difficult for her to decide.

I was not involved in any discussions and certainly had no say in her eventual decision to stay. We were never a touchy-feely-lets-talk-it-all-over type of family. I was not consulted but I think in the end my mother just thought she did not want to uproot me and herself from our lives in cosy old Bradford, Manchester. I guess the bottom line was that she just did not love Norman enough to make such a colossal move and change in her life. I think she thought of me, to be honest. That was the only boyfriend my mother had ever had and it was always very difficult. My grandma refused to look after me sometimes because she thought my mother might be going out to meet another man. Years later my mum told me she had always found it very hard to get out because my grandma flatly refused to babysit me. My grandma wanted my mother to cook and clean like she always had done but she certainly did not want her to find another husband and have any kind of life for herself. It sounds a bit selfish and cruel and in a way it was. But I suppose while my mother was there with me it was helping to keep the memory alive for my grandma of the son she had lost.

Families all have their secrets and ours was no different. My mother told me before she died that my father used to send parcels home from whichever country he was in. When my mother got home from work she would inevitably find they had already been opened by my grandmother and all the gifts inside had been given out. And my auntie Vera to this day wears an 'Aries' necklace that was sent for me by my dad. Vera was not born under the star sign Aries, but I was. My mother was not really part of their family so she had no say and she was simply sidelined by my grandma. It must have been an incredibly difficult time for my mother but she never ever opened up to me about it all, even when she was old and living in Blackpool.

My mother put up with some quite unkind behaviour from my grandmother for years and years. She used to have to do Ninny's feet, not the other girls. And she also had to do all the baking, and any other jobs around the house that my grandma wanted doing. My grandfather might have ruled the household, but my grandmother ruled the lives of her two daughters and of my mother.

My grandfather could be scary but he was not a violent man. He worked on the roads and he used to travel all over the country. One night he came in really angry and I saw glimpses of a vicious temper. He was absolutely furious because he had broken his arm and I was terrified of what he might do. But he was just angry because it meant he could not work and earn a living. There were no benefits in those days. Normally he was a very quiet man, and just lived for his family and his game of dominoes. He didn't like drink and so he never went into a pub and he always said that because of that, he missed out on sharing the sociability of his lads. There were so many happy family occasions and I was always a bridesmaid at my aunties' and uncles' weddings.

After poor rejected Norman had gone off to Rhodesia alone my mum started going out with a man called Joseph Donovan. He was a tall, red-haired Irishman who was quite a character, I suppose. They would go to the pictures or out for a drink and all of a sudden my mother had another interest in her life apart from me. I suppose I must have been jealous although I honestly cannot recall feeling resentment that I had a rival for my mother's affections. When she was courting Joe, a girl called May Jones used to look after me. She was only a bit older than me, about 16 I suppose, but she was old enough to be trusted. She would come and stay with me when my mother went out with Joe. My mother and I had a row once at this time and I remember I said 'You like May Jones more than you like me.' I didn't really mean May Jones. What I really meant was that she liked Joe more than me, but that was such an awful thing I could not bring myself to say it out loud like that. I think that was the only thing I ever said to her about Joe and even then I didn't use his name. I never asked about her relationship with Joe or her plans or anything. Today I'm sure mother and daughter would have lots of deep and meaningful discussions about their feelings and the future and everything. But it wasn't like that in my day and in my family. I didn't have the knowledge or the confidence to ask the questions.

My new stepfather was completely different to my mother. While she was very shy and withdrawn he was quite outgoing and used to sing in pubs sometimes. Before the wedding day my mother bought me all these new clothes to wear for the big occasion but I refused to go and I went youth hostelling with my friends instead! I suppose I was quite wilful and even then I knew my own mind but I didn't snub the wedding out of spite. The youth hostelling trip to the Lake District came on the same day as my mum's wedding and at the time it felt like that trip with my mates was much more important to me than my mum's wedding. We stayed in a youth hostel in Kendal and when I got back my mum had a husband and he was living with her in our house. They did not go away on a honeymoon. They just got married and after the weekend he went back to work and so did she. He didn't move in until the day they got married; you didn't do that back in those days. That really would have been shocking.

And when I came home I brought some of my friends back to sleep at our house so I would not have to be at home with just my mum and her new husband. I was in a bedroom of my own and I brought my mates back. We never called them sleepovers then but I suppose that was what it was. I never even thought about the sexual side of my mum being with a man after all these years. That was not in my mind. Today kids might think 'my mum is having sex with her new man'

32

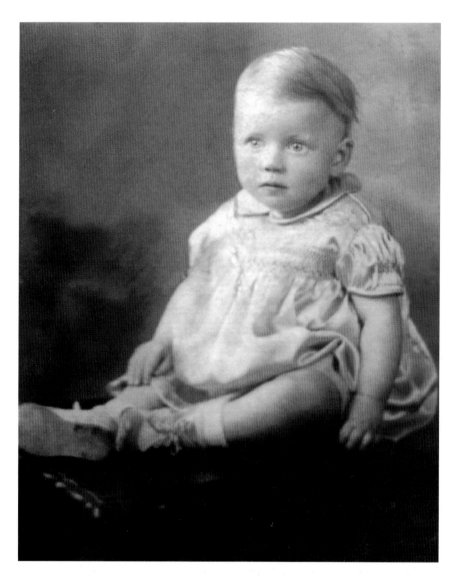

Baby Patricia Talbot, pictured in 1939

Street party, 1950
That's me right in the front, eating an ice cream

Manchester Whit Walk

In my Whit Walk dress (far left) with classmates at St. Bridget's

On holiday with the family in Blackpool

Me as a keen young Irish dancer in 1952

Outside the house in John Street, Bradford

My first marriage to Harry Whittaker, December 1956

Signing the register with Harry after our wedding ceremony

Rudi and me on our first trip to Blackpool together

Rudi in borrowed uniform in 1942

because everything is so explicit. It was not about sex, it was just that she had got married and there was a strange man in the house and I decided I wanted to have my mates there.

There was nothing wrong with Joe Donovan. In fact in many ways he was very nice. He was a scaffolder in the building game and after work his entertainment was heading straight for the pub and having a few pints. He came home when the pub shut at half past ten, but my mother was a good cook and she prepared a lovely meal for him every night. That was her prize. She would bake a proper sweet as well.

My mum getting married did change my life. Pretty soon my mum became pregnant although she never ever talked to me about it. Eventually it simply became obvious and my brother Paul was born without my mother and I ever having a single conversation about the new situation at home. She worked until shortly before the birth. After Paul had arrived I went up to the hospital to see the newest member of the family. I was looking forward to this baby coming and I really wanted a brother. I wanted to have someone I could put in a pram and wheel about. But when I saw him I was shocked. He looked like a horrible little monkey. But he soon improved and by the time he came home I thought he was gorgeous. I tried to help her with the household jobs but when I did the washing I made a mistake and put something pink in with the whites and all Joe's underwear came out pink. I begged to be allowed to take out my little brother in his pram but then I left him at the shops and forgot all about him and came home alone. I'd completely forgotten I'd got a brother. When my mother asked where he was I realised what I'd done and dashed back and he was still in the chemist's. They were more innocent times then but I was still very worried that someone might have taken him. But really I thought it was marvellous to have a brother and I took him everywhere I could.

I was at the age where I was beginning to develop as a woman. My bust was starting to arrive, and I was getting to like myself a little bit and starting to take an interest in doing my hair. It had been just me and my mum for so long it felt very strange to have another person in the house, especially a man. I had been used to wandering around in anything and all of a sudden I had to be more careful if I was just in my underwear. Not that he ever did anything dodgy but nothing was the same any more. I did slowly get used to him but I did feel sorry for my mum making his dinner and him staying out late in the pub with his mates drinking. He was not a violent man in any way. She was the one that shouted because she was so mad that he wasn't there for dinner.

3

Boys

Iwas 14 when I had my first boyfriend. By the standards of today I was very shy and backward with boys but then I think we all were. Lads were just friends to play with mainly in those days. It was illegal to gamble then and the men used to play pitch and toss and we used to get tuppence for keeping watch in case the police came round. It seemed pretty harmless even then.

Bonfire Night was an event of great excitement. I loved it. But it was the only time in my young life that I got into any real trouble. I joined the lads in a raid on a wood yard. I was a real tomboy in those days. I wore jeans a lot and a plaid shirt, that was my playing out gear. Most of the other girls wore dresses but I preferred to look like a boy, in my early teens at least. I was definitely more of a lad than a girl. I always wanted to be with the lads, playing their games. I loved their games more than I liked girls games. I got into trouble for climbing over the fence of this wood yard and stealing crates to burn on our bonfire.

My granddad was furious when he found out what I had been doing and he dragged me to Mill Street police station. I was screaming my head off as we went. It was probably about half a mile and I got more and more scared with every step he took. We got to the steps at the front of the building and I could see inside through the glass doors that there was a big policeman standing behind a desk and I was absolutely terrified that I was going to be taken in and locked up for the rest of my life. My grandad took me onto the steps and I thought I had really had it this time and he stopped and said, 'Now then, the next time you steal anything, you will be going in there'. The terrifying feeling of the fear I felt has stayed with me to this day. My granddad hated stealing and dishonesty of any kind and he was genuinely very angry with me. It might have been only an old wooden crate I stole but it could have been the Queen's diamond necklace to my granddad. He was absolutely straight down the line with his principles and he was passionately against theft. 'You don't steal anything, ever,' he shouted at me. I thought, 'It was only a bit of blinking wood that probably nobody wanted anyway,' but I got the message loud and clear. I don't think I've stolen a single thing since. It still makes me go cold to think about how completely filled with fear I was that day.

I was always a bit of a squealer because I was a bit spoilt by all my aunts and uncles when I was growing up. I was the only grandchild. Nobody else had had a baby, only my dad. So all the attention off these adults did sometimes go to my head if I'm honest. I used to squeal if I wanted anything and then usually I got it. I remember being in Woolworth's once, the one in Oldham Street that burned down, and there were these big staircases with bold brass banisters sweeping down and all the way up and from the top you could see down three floors. I took my hat off and threw it right down to the bottom because I was squealing my head off for something and I was not getting the attention I thought I deserved. I just let it drop and I was in trouble again.

My granddad was very strict and although I didn't get into trouble that many times I can remember all of them. One day we were playing May Queens, dressing up in our back yard. We were only putting on old rags. There was this girl across the road who was being dressed up so of course we had to undress her first. There was no sexual side to any of this on my life, it was all totally innocent. We had lit candles and this girl got candle wax on her neck and her face and her mother saw it. Her mother was not too impressed and stormed over demanding to know what was going on in our back yard. I got pinged for it.

My granddad took me upstairs and tied my hand to the rail on this bed. He said 'You will stay there all day'. I was left all day tied up which looking back I suppose was not a very nice punishment but at the end of the day I just laughed and said, 'I enjoyed that granddad, why don't you do it again sometime.' At the time I thought it was a game like cowboys and indians. He just had to laugh and really I was spoiled for most of my life. I never got hit. My best friend got the belt and lots of others did as well. I was always dressed well because my mother worked as a passer in Barracuta, a big clothing manufacturer in Beswick Street in Ancoats. She used to take me in to work on a Saturday because she often had to work overtime after she became a passer.

My mother never told me a single thing about sex. It was one of the many things we did not talk about. When my periods began it was five days before I could tell her. I told my friend about this strange sensation and the bleeding and my friend told her mum and her mum told my mum. And I got a crack across the head and the sanitary towels were put in the drawer and that was my sexual education! That was it, baby! And I was wearing four pairs of navy blue knickers that I had pinched from school for a week. I was 15 years old when I started my periods. Everybody else had started long before me. I thought there was something wrong with me. I'll never forget the moment they began. I was just coming out of the Don cinema on Sunday afternoon. I thought 'Why am I all wet?' I was so naïve I didn't know what was happening until I got home. I was glad in a way because all my friends had started when they were 13 or 14.

My first boyfriend was a lad called Raymond Massey. I went out with him for about a year and a half. He's dead now poor chap, but his wife is still living and she's been here to the Queens Hotel. I met him at cookery classes of all places.

We had to go to Queen Street School for cookery because there were no facilities at St Bridget's. We just spent one day a week up there, usually baking. It was a mixed Protestant school so that was a bit of a change on two fronts. I was confronted with unassailable proof that differences of both gender and religion existed and needed to be dealt with. Also it took me out of my own familiar areas and away from the mates I had known since I was a kid. But gradually the new faces became a definite attraction. I don't think I would have considered any of the boys from our street as a boyfriend because I already knew them much too well. We had grown up together so somehow I knew them too well to think they might be potential boyfriend material.

I'm not trying to be Miss Prim but in those days I honestly had no thoughts of sex in my mind. I know some people might find that hard to believe but it's true. It just wasn't that kind of thing when I met Raymond for the first time. It was so fresh and different from any boy I'd been friendly with before. It started when he came up and began talking to me. I'm not an idiot, I knew he liked me and I liked him. Then he started carrying my cakes home from school. Sometimes we would stop and spend time together in the park eating cakes and we slowly became closer. I remember getting home one day and my mum couldn't understand why I'd not brought any cakes home and it was because me and Raymond Massey had eaten them in the park. We were both only 14 and he used to have a paper round on a Saturday night, taking round the *Football Extra*. After he had finished I used to meet up with him and on the way home we would stand in a back entry together. It was still very innocent but we did kiss each other and he would put his hand on my breasts, outside my clothes of course, and cuddle me. That's what you did in those days. I suppose I was too scared to go any further and I'm pretty sure he was as well. We carried on like that for about a year, until I was 15 and a half.

Then I started work and of course I met a whole new lot of people and my horizons were instantly widened. I left school on the Friday and started work on the Monday and my life was changed forever. I started going to dance halls. There was not much choice of career for girls like me. They took me to C & A and to the local coal mine, Bradford Pit at the top of the street where most people's dads worked. It wasn't work experience, they just took you out for the day to show you the two alternatives for people like us. Can you imagine that? I was not impressed by the Pit, but I saw this girl working in an office at a coalyard in Ashton Hall Road and that part of it didn't look too bad. So I just said I'd like to work at the office. I wasn't that keen really, but I hadn't passed any exams and I wasn't that interested to go anywhere. I might not have had the intelligence to pass exams but I knew I wasn't a dummy at school. For most of my time at school I came fourth or fifth or sixth. I was never the brains of the class but I wasn't down the bottom.

I earned about £2 a week at the coalyard office and I used to hand it all over to my mother and she used to give me 10 bob back! I felt so grown up when I handed over my money to my mother. But I didn't stay at the coalyard very long. It was grubby and dirty there, even in the office. I got a job filing at John England's which was part of Great Universal Stores and fell in with a whole new gang of friends who brightened up my social life no end.

We started going dancing on a Saturday night to Chick Hibbert's. It was fabulous fun and a whole new world opened. We used to love jiving. There was no drink or drugs in our lives, we seemed to get excited enough just jiving! As soon as I got my high heels on there was no holding me. I thought I was the bee's knees. And I had to rush out and meet Raymond after he had done his papers on Barmouth Street. He would always be standing there but sometimes I used to let him down and he would realise I had been dancing. He was not happy about that and he packed me in.

There was no messing about or second chances; he just completely packed me in. I was so distraught at the time I used to cry myself to sleep every night. One of the big hit songs of the day was *Answer Me* by David Whitfield and I used to put it on the record player and cry to it every night because he had left me in the lurch. I used to go back to our favourite meeting place but he just never came again. I was very upset, for several weeks at least.

When you're 15 you get over things pretty fast. It was the end of my first relationship with a boy and it was totally without sex. We did used to press ourselves closely together in our most passionate moments in the alley but that's as far as it ever got. I did feel the awakening of sexual feelings but I was much too frightened of getting pregnant to do anything about it. I was brought up in different times. I can't remember a single girl in our school every getting pregnant and I bet there is not a girl in the land who can truthfully say that these days. But the very thought of getting pregnant scared me stiff. It was not that I didn't know about sex at that age. I had learned what I imagined to be the basics from the other girls at school but I was never one of the most forward in that department.

But I did start to take more of an interest in fashion. All my fifties and sixties gear is now in fashion again. Vanity cases had just come out and flat shoes that we used to buy off the market for 9/11 have all come back. We used to get a split skirt and stockings off the market. They were cheaper if they were damaged. Sometimes you got three butterflies up one side and two down the other, but who cared if you saved a few pennies. I thought I looked really smart in that with my black sweater and we used to walk around with growing confidence as if we looked terrific.

Not that we ever veered off the straight and narrow. In those days life was very simple. You got up and went to work and you couldn't wait to go jiving at night. And you were knackered at half past ten because you had to get up so early to go to work. I loved going to dance halls with my friends. There was a gang of about five or six of us who used to just love dancing the night away. I lived in an almost totally white world when I was young. There was just one black girl who used to hang round with us. She was called Rita and I met her at Chick Hibbert's and I used to love jiving with her because she was a great dancer. We used to go in competitions together and sometimes we won them. I can't ever remember anyone saying anything about her colour. It never mattered to Rita and it certainly never mattered to us.

My new career did not last long. I was sacked from John England's for something I thought was pretty trivial. There were 20 of us in a section in a massive big long room. Our section head was a man called Mr Spellercy. Every day we used to go to get fish and chips for everyone on our section. Lunch was at twelve o'clock and we started going early so we could get back in time with everyone's lunch. We had such a big order that one morning we left at quarter past eleven because we knew otherwise by the time we got back we would have no time for lunch. We were coming back with this great big tray and we were seen by Mr Isherwood, one of the bosses. Then after lunch we were asked to go to Mr Spellercy. He didn't beat about the bush and just said, 'You're fired'. We were shocked and asked why. He said because you were seen outside at quarter past eleven. We said our fish and chip order is that big that if we don't go early we will miss our lunch. 'You're fired,' he said. He hardly went down as one of my favourite people and I was to meet him years later when his wife was in the hairdresser's and they had a small boarding house and I was in the Queens Hotel. I didn't dare tell him because I didn't think he'd ever remember me.

Then a friend said she had a good job at Robinson's jam works. I think I was on £5.50 a week and it seemed like good money. Three of us who got sacked all started there at once. We used to get the bus to Droylesden together and it was like a new adventure even if we were just on a production line picking the jam pots off. I couldn't believe that I was earning all this money, but I still ran home and gave my mum all the money.

After a while I left because I didn't like the job. It was very noisy all the time and I thought I was going deaf. And I hated the work. We had to wear these awful overalls and every now and then a girl would get badly scalded with hot jam. But I stuck it for a few weeks because it was good money. And when I left I got this surprising chunk of money. It must have been a tax rebate but it was a really nice moment. Once again though, I just gave it all to my mother. She did give me some back but I was so sure handing over everything was the right thing to do.

4

Teenage Bride

Dancing at the Palais helped to heal my broken heart and quite soon after Raymond's rejection I met the man who was to become my first husband. There I was, minding my own business, just going down Albert Street to get the bus and, as I went to get on, I noticed this tall lad looking at me. He said 'Where yer off?' I said, 'I'm going to Chick's' and he said, 'I'm going there'. But I didn't stop, I just carried on walking and got on the bus. I didn't really think anything more of it but later that night he came up and asked me for a dance. And later he took me home.

I was 16 and he was 21. He was called Harry Whittaker and like my stepfather, he worked as a scaffolder. He was a very good looking guy. Not just tall, but dark and handsome as well. I remember he reminded me of Burt Lancaster and Richard Conti. He had a Teddy boy haircut and a very nice smile. What more could girl ask for? I fell in love with him.

As it turned out I didn't just get a new boyfriend, before long I got a new career as well, because Harry's mother helped me to find a new job. She used to go to this hairdresser who was looking for an assistant. I had never even considered hairdressing as a career but I needed a job so I took it. I started by washing hair and from that moment I found something I liked doing. It wasn't just the washing and the other menial jobs I was landed with at first, it was the whole feel of the job. I liked the customers and I liked the place. I loved chatting with people about their lives and as I learned the trade I knew I had found something I could do and do well. I'm not saying I wanted to perm people's hair for the rest of my life but I knew I had found something I could do and a way I could always earn a living. It gave me at that young age a feeling of independence that I have never lost. The hairdresser was a nice lady called Elsie Pierce and soon she trusted me to look after the shop in Ashton Hall Road when she wasn't there. She became more of a friend than a boss and she came to my wedding. She bought me a pressure cooker and that was a big wedding present. I was very grateful. I worked there a long time.

Sex reared its head pretty early in my relationship with Harry. I was still young but I had grown up a little. The trouble was that there was never anywhere to go to actually sleep together, but it went a bit further than it had with Raymond. We touched and caressed each other but never went all the way until we went away to Blackpool together. Not for the last time that town played an important part in my life. Harry and I got some holiday together and headed for the seaside. We stayed in a little place in Chapel Street, just near Madame Tussaud's where the train used to run. It's all been pulled down long ago.

We booked two single rooms, as you had to in those days, but he used to sneak into my room late at night and we slept together at last. It was very exciting, particularly as it was against all the rules of the day. At one point someone knocked on the door and he leapt into the wardrobe! We were dead scared. I'm not sure what we thought might happen to us, but we were absolutely terrified that we might be found out. That was when I had sex for the first time.

And then we went for a weekend in London together when I was still only 17. We travelled to London on the train and had sex there again and after that we did it wherever and whenever we could manage it. So I did have sex before we were married which was still a big taboo in those days.

There was a big difference in our ages I suppose but we seemed to get on well. We had the usual courtship and so on and ended up getting married. To be fair it was a great courtship and a great everything. We couldn't get enough of each other. We just longed to be together.

In fact in one of the weird coincidences that seem to keep occurring in my life, when we were courting Harry almost introduced me to Rudi Mancini. We were already engaged when he took me to one of Rudi's pubs and I could have met the man who was later to change my life so enormously. I had this black dress on and a long string of pearls I got off the market and high heels of course. And to mark our engagement he took me out for a drink to a pub called the Kings' Arms on Ancoat's Lane and I walked in and I can remember the layout to this day. There was a bar over to one side and a dark woman behind the bar. You went out through a door and there was a long room and at the top of this long room there was a wall and a stage and we sat right at the very bottom on seats at the very end. There was a big, white organ there with mirrors round it. It was an entertainments place and this fella came and played the organ, and that was Rudi. I never spoke to him, or even exchanged a glance as far as I can remember, but he was there, the night I got engaged. That was Rudi's wife sat behind the bar. When you look back, it's spooky.

So Harry and I decided to get married even though I was only 17. It didn't feel too young to me. Girls did get married younger in those days. People didn't move in together; my mother and the rest of my family would have been devastated if I'd done that. But Harry was a Protestant and I was a Catholic so he couldn't get married in a Catholic church back in those dark days. We got married in his church, St Barnabas in Openshaw. First we went to see the priest and he gave us a lecture about caring for each other in good times and bad. He gravely advised us that when things became difficult and we found ourselves considering breaking up the marriage we must be steadfast and stick together.

When we came out after listening to that we ran down the street laughing. We said, 'Did you hear all that. "If we leave each other" stuff. How could we ever even think of splitting up?' We were so much in love that the very idea was absolutely unthinkable. I was just madly in love with him. There was nothing else like him. I couldn't wait to get married and I was totally convinced I would be Mrs Whittaker for the rest of my life.

When it came to arranging the wedding I was very clear on one thing. I was not going to let my stepfather Joe give me away. Was that a bit mean? Looking back perhaps it was, but I insisted my grandfather gave me away because he had been like a father to me for so long. I saved up for ages and bought this wonderful dress from Affleck and Brown, in Manchester.

I was determined to be a proper home-maker and we got a little house. It was just another typical two-up and two-down terraced house in Thomas Street in the nearby suburb of Gorton. It cost £250 and we were desperate to buy it rather than renting. So we put a few quid down as a deposit. I can't remember if it was £20 or £30 but it was enough to secure the house and we moved in. We had saved up to buy a few bits of furniture but it did not take much to fill it. It was only a very small house. You walked in from the street and you were in the living room and there was just the kitchen in the back. But we loved it.

In fact I saw Rudi another time, after I was married. I got the 53 bus to Oldham Road from Gorton and went into the Cheshire Cheese with some friends from work. There was a man playing a big white organ and it was Rudi. Drags acts were on including my old friend Frank who was now known as Foo Foo Lamar; Neville Sinclair, Penny Lane, it was quite a night. Rudi and I talked about it years later. Our paths crossed but neither of us realised it.

My mum was all in favour of us getting married. We planned everything really carefully. We used to order stuff for the house and store it all at home ready for our big day. My mum's house got so full of our carpets and tables and chairs and stuff that she used to complain 'Look at the state of my house. There is no room to swing a cat.' But she didn't mind really. I think she liked Harry and she thought we were being sensible and going about things the right way. I was full of myself and was busily saving up money for my wedding frock in one envelope, money for the bridesmaids' frocks in another envelope and money for the car in another. I was very determined and very organised. And at first we were really happy together. I was madly in love with him. Absolutely head over heels. Five years is quite a big age difference when you're only 17 but I've always been attracted to the older man. Raymond was the same age as me but that was never serious. Harry was the man I wanted to spend the rest of my life with. He was kind and protective and I loved him. I thought we'd be together forever. He had been in the Army and had served in Korea so he was much more of a man of the world than anyone I had ever known before.

We had planned to get married in August because we both wanted a summer wedding. But my mother became pregnant with my sister Sharron and she asked us to delay the wedding. She had already given birth to my brother Paul and now she was having another baby with Joe. I was devastated because all my plans had been made so carefully and I was really looking forward to my big day. My mother simply could not face going on the wedding photographs looking pregnant. She was very shy and she felt it was something to be embarrassed about. Nowadays I'm sure no-one would give the pregnancy of the bride's mother a second thought but these were very different times. We put the wedding back to December 14.

We didn't have a honeymoon. We had already spent every penny we had in setting up our home and we wouldn't have dreamed of going into debt to pay for a holiday in those days. We just went straight to the house and got on with being man and wife. It was a fabulous feeling having a place of your own with the man you love. I might have been only 17 years old but I felt as if I had grown up at last. We both went back to work on the Monday and everything in the garden was rosy. Except we didn't have a garden, just a backyard, but you know what I mean. Life was wonderful for quite a while. Harry enjoyed being newlywed just as much as I did and he would dash home straight from work and we would do what newlyweds do. We were both very much in love with each other and we enjoyed the freedom to explore the physical side of our relationship.

But gradually Harry started coming home a bit late for his dinner. He liked going for a drink with his mates after work and over a period of time, a couple of quick drinks turned into a whole night out. I wanted very much to be a good wife and I always prepared a lovely meal for us, every night without fail. He began coming home later and later. He was always still in his scruffy donkey jacket from work, so I was sure he had not been with another woman.

Now I knew what my mother had to put up with with my stepfather. After a while it became most nights of the week I would be left waiting as the dinner went cold. He never used to come home until 11o'clock. He never ran around after other women, he just couldn't resist going to the pub with the lads. It was very frustrating. I was a good cleaner and cook and I also became very house proud. I would make our tea and get the table ready for him coming home at six. I used to collect a few strawberries in the summer and try to make everything nice. But I would sit watching the clock for hours and he just never could get home on time. He always had to stay in the pub. At 11 he would eventually come in. He was not drunk, just a little bit the worse for wear, and I was never a battered wife but he would shout and moan and be in a bad mood. He had to get out of the pub at half past ten in those days. There were no nightclubs to go to in our area.

That behaviour ate away at the love between us and started a horrible rift. We would argue bitterly as I have never been the sort of person afraid from speaking my mind. The rows got worse and after a particularly angry bust-up I stormed out and left him and went back to my mother's. I never went back in that house again, but he came round and apologised and we got back together but I still refused to go back to that house.

Then my mother found out that a house round the corner from where she lived was empty and it was going to be coming up for sale. We went after it straight away because it had a lean-to at the back and all the yard was covered by a glass roof that meant the toilet was inside the house which was considered a great luxury in those days. It had been beautifully converted and we managed somehow to get the money together again and bought it and moved in together again.

Harry promised he would not stay in the pub all night and for a time he was better but after a while he slipped back into his old ways. He just couldn't see the harm in it but I found it heart-breaking to have slaved over putting together a romantic meal for two, only to be left to eat it alone.

There was just the two of us for three years and I started to think I wouldn't be able to have kids. But when I was 20 I became pregnant which was great news for both of us. Pregnancy sort of patched up the rift between us for a while. We did still care for each other and we both wanted to have a family, but we were hardly love's young dream any longer.

I had our son Dean in Crumsall Hospital and in those days the visiting times were very limited. You could have only one person to visit for one hour and that was it. When you've just had your first baby you desperately want your husband to come and see you and your son. This was long before husbands were encouraged to be there to share in the birth. I had Dean at eight o'clock in the morning. It was February 1961 and I went into hospital the night before when I went into labour and the midwife told me straight away that I wouldn't give birth until eight o'clock next morning. She was spot on. I'd never been in hospital before in my life so I was frightened half to death and I did not know what to expect

But once baby Dean arrived everything changed. I was so proud of our little newborn son and I was so looking forward to a visit from Harry that night. But, at visiting time, while every other mother and baby had a beaming father arriving to share the magical moment, Harry never came. I'll never forget lying in that ward waiting, watching the door frantically hoping he had just been delayed, but he never came. I was the only one in the ward who did not have a visitor. I hid my head under the bedclothes I was so upset. I cried and I cried. It was awful. He had gone straight to the pub from work, got pissed, and he never came. I was devastated. My mother went mad because she could have come and visited if he'd said he wasn't coming. Next day he came with flowers and the usual meaningless apologies. He had meant to come of course but he had started celebrating with his mates, wetting the baby's head, and somehow his visit had got forgotten.

I was very angry and felt let down. But I came home and tried to get over it. As soon as I was well enough to go back to work I used to put Dean in a nursery every day and go off to work. We needed the money and I wanted to work. And I soon got pregnant again. This time, in May 1962, I had Pamela, our daughter. The birth was at home. We had two lovely children, born 15 months apart, but only one of us seemed to take responsibility for them. All the neighbours used to come in and visit and I was full of hopes that things would change, but my husband was still suffering from a bad case of bottle fatigue.

For a long time I tried to put a brave face on the troubles in my marriage. I was very close to my mum but I tried not to burden her with my problems. I'd talk about the weather, or her work, anything to avoid my boozing husband. When I was a passer with my mum at the Peter England shirt factory in Ardwick Green, Manchester, she used to hate doing stuff for Marks and Spencer because they used to send inspectors round and if they saw a mistake or a piece of cotton loose they would just say 'I don't want that' and reject it on sight. They were very picky, M & S.

After a while I used to go as passer there, just checking everything. It was decent wages so I went full-time. But my life became a grind. I loved the kids but my husband was always in the pub. Once a week I used to get up at six o'clock in the morning, go to the wash-house to scrub all the clothes because we had no washing machine, wrap 'em all, get my husband up and off for work and then get the kids up and take them to the nursery or, later, to school, and then go off to work myself. Times were very different. Girls of today who are the age I was then still can't boil a bleeding egg! I'm not saying I should be put on a pedestal for it. No, no, no. A lot of women did it in those days. A lot of families needed the woman's wage just to exist so the kids would be taken to a relative or to the nursery so that the woman could go off to work. And without the labour saving devices of today it was damned hard work. It was part and parcel of working class life in those days. It was what was expected of you, so you did it.

Harry tried to be a good husband and father but usually the lure of the pub was too strong for him to arrive home before closing time. I used to sit, with my babies, waiting. I knew it was my mother's experience with Joe all over again. But I was not my mother. Deep down I knew I would not put up with this behaviour for ever. He knew I couldn't go out myself because I was stuck at home looking after the children and he seemed to think it was his right, as a man and the breadwinner, to stay out as late as he liked and drink as much as he wanted. That is when our relationship began to become really difficult.

As the months went by I became gradually more and more disenchanted with my situation. He never ever came home on time. In some ways he was still a good husband. He gave me every penny of his wage packet. He used to slap it on the table and I would give him money back to get to work and so on. He was marvellous with our children, always, I can't fault him there. But even so the marriage really started to deteriorate and our relationship became unhappy. He never hit me, unlike many husbands, but he did push me once, when I was pregnant with Pamela, and I still have a bent finger to prove it. He shoved me over a chair and up against the wall quite hard. That was all the violence he ever showed towards me. We were having a row and he flared up and I just looked at him and said, 'One day you'll be sorry you've done that.' I don't know why I said it but at the time I knew it was true.

I was just frustrated that whatever I did to try to make our life as nice as possible made no difference to what time he came home from the pub. I would try to brighten up our evening meal by putting a vase of flowers on the table. Not that I was even a little bit posh, but I just wanted things to look nice. Everything was clean and the kids had two painted drawers from an old sideboard with the names 'Pamela' and 'Dean' on them. I used to boil all the nappies up in the backyard to get them clean as soon as I could to make them look white. I always used to spend a lot of money on clothes for the kids. I would say that was one of my weaknesses. I would go to a shop in Eccles where they had this French stuff, beautiful and stylish clothes for kids. Not all the time, just for special occasions but I really cared and tried to make our lives as perfect as possible. I did all the right things but he still didn't come home until the pub shut. It wasn't every night he was late but a lot of nights. Sometimes I would be looking in the paper to see if there had been an accident because being a scaffolder sometimes he had to work on very high and dangerous buildings. Every night he came home late we would have a row and it would end up with him promising he would never do it again. And at the time, because he promised me, I believed him. And then I would be scouring the paper or even ringing the hospital to see if a mishap at work had injured him.

It got so bad between us that I would take his money and not give him anything back so he couldn't go in the pub. But they used to get private jobs at night to board up a premises that had been broken into or whatever, that they used to call 'ghosters', and for those they would be paid in cash. Or they would flog aluminium, the 'alloy' as they called it, so he had his own ways of getting money to go and buy drink. Sometimes he did have to walk to work in the morning because I just wouldn't hand over the money. He would stand there pleading, 'I just want my bus fare' and I would flatly refuse saying he couldn't have any bus fare because he might walk to work and then use his fare to buy beer. Many a time he was forced to walk to work but it never, ever stopped him from drinking. It sounds funny when I remember the stories of all the rows but it definitely was not funny at the time.

When it got really bad between the two of us he would leave me and go and stay at his mother's house. It happened when we were christening Dean at the big church and Harry never turned up. He missed his own son's christening. It still makes me angry all these years later. I went to his mother's house the day before and knocked on the door but he still wouldn't come. The relationship really went downhill after that.

On the day of Pamela's christening, I told him 'You've come to your daughter's christening but you never went to your son's'. It was a niggling relationship that went from bad to worse. I don't know whether I had fallen out of love with him or what. We were just in a routine of him coming in late and us rowing about drink. It's all we ever rowed about but it was enough to drive us apart.

5

Freedom And Infidelity

The marriage got worse and I got a job in the town. A friend of mine said there was a cabaret club in town that was looking for staff. The pay was £10 a night just for standing there! It sounded too good to be true. So I said, 'Get us an interview'. My husband promised to be home from work in time to mind the kids on the day of my interview but not surprisingly he didn't turn up.

I persuaded my friend to watch them so she put them to bed and just sat with them. So I went for this interview and the guy's name was Alan Kay. He and his brother had the Cabaret Club on Oxford Street in Manchester. It was a very glamorous place. They used to have singers on like Matt Monro and comedians like Bob Monkhouse. I was very impressed. It was a gambling casino as well and to me it was just the height of sophistication. I put on my best black dress with its scoop neck for the interview and I had my hair down and I thought I really looked good. I was very excited. I went into this room and said I was applying for a job.

Alan Kay said the vacancy they had was for a hostess. Now a hostess to me did not mean a prostitute. If they said you were a working girl it might mean you were on the game but it did not mean that to me. I was told that I just had to stand and be pleasant with the customers and if anyone did not want you standing with them then you just had to move off sharpish. But if someone wants your company while they're on a winning streak then that's your job. If they think you're bringing them some good fortune then you stick around. That was the job. Well, after the coalyard and the jam factory that sounded like money for old rope. The job was 'Just look nice and make the punters think you're lucky'. I thought that doesn't sound too difficult.

Then he said, 'I need to look at your legs!' My dress was up to my knees and I didn't really like the sound of that idea but I hitched my dress up higher than my knees so he could have a look. He said 'Higher' and I hitched it up a little more. He said 'Higher' and I raised it another inch. He said 'Higher' and I said, 'I am going no higher'. I was not going to start getting my clothes off for this man who was a lot older than me. There was a moment when I thought I'd blown my chances but he just smiled and said, 'You've got the job'. Of course that was the start of a whole new phase in my life. Previously I had been trapped at home looking after the kids every night. My husband stayed in the pub night after night, downing pint after pint, secure in the knowledge that I was at home looking after his kids. But not any more.

He was a bit surprised when I told him I would be going out to work till very late some nights and he would be required for babysitting duties. But the money I was to earn was very good and we desperately needed it. All of a sudden I had a glamorous new development in my previously dull and predictable life. It was fun in the casino where everyone was well dressed and confident. I was good with people, I always have been and I even think that more than once I was lucky for some of the punters. Who knows? It hardly mattered so long as they thought my sweet smile made the odds on them going home a winner a little better everyone was happy. Except my husband of course who found that his drinking was curtailed by my absence, though he often sneaked out of the job by recruiting a babysitter or persuading my mother to take care of them.

It wasn't all a laugh a minute at the Cabaret Club, but I started to learn a lot about life. One night I was taking a drink in for Matt Monro when I was intercepted by a hard-faced woman, caked in make-up, who demanded to know where I was going. She insisted on taking the drink from me. I realised later that she was probably a prostitute but in any case she took my chance of meeting a star from me at the very last minute. I was hardly bothered because I was enjoying the fantastic freedom of working in the Cabaret Club. We used to work till the early hours and then everybody moved off to have breakfast at an all-night café called Nikki's. I had money to buy new clothes and the work as a hostess was hardly arduous. I knew when to smile and I could chat to people. I soon discovered that most of them were lonely and ready enough to have a chat with a friendly face.

There was never any impropriety involved at any time. There was certainly no shagging on my part; I was still a very good girl. But in any case, to me there was a strange innocence about the place. In spite of it being a sinister night club full of dodgy people, I just found that the men were there to gamble. I'm not saying that there were no illicit sexual encounters from time to time but I wasn't involved. I became very friendly with a couple of girls there and none of us did anything more than try to bring the punters some good luck. But for me it was liberating. The only night life I had seen before was at Chick Hibbert's dance palace which was not nearly so stylish.

It brought a total change to my life. I still had the same daily grinding routine of being a working mother but now, also, several times a week, I had the excitement of going off into a thrilling new world which was an awful lot more fun than waiting up to yell angrily at my husband for spending another night in the pub. I was in the night scene of the hottest club in Manchester earning £10 a night, which was a lot of money in those days. We went to Nikki's early one morning for breakfast and there was a guy there who asked me what I did for a living. I tried to explain and he shocked me when he said, 'Do you fancy coming with me on a date?'

I was totally stunned. I was a married woman after all, even if my marriage was hardly love's young dream any longer. He said he worked for Express Newspapers in Ancoat's Lane, Manchester, in the famous big black glass building. 'I'm in and out all night so I could meet you in a club up there called the Ponderosa if you like', he said. I agreed. We arranged to meet at eight o'clock on my night off, when my husband thought I was hard at work. I met him and he took me into this scruffy club, with a late licence. There was a bald man in there with a big belt round his trousers, who was bustling round cleaning all the tables. I didn't take much notice but that was Rudi Mancini. He owned the place.

This fellow I was with kept bobbing in and out to work and this bald man took a break from cleaning the tables and talked to me. 'Who are you with?' he asked. I was Miss Prim. I was 24 and he was a lot older. I found out later he was 20 years older. He was 44. But he asked me out. I was a bit surprised because he looked like an old man to me. I agreed to meet him but I never even turned up. I stood him up and I did feel awful about it. A couple of weeks later I was in there again with this other bloke and Rudi was cleaning the tables. When I had the chance I had to say something I just blurted out, 'I'm sorry I didn't turn up the other night but I'm married with a couple of kids'.

I felt terrible for standing him up. At the time, although my marriage was unhappy, I really wasn't looking for another man. I think I felt safe with Rudi! He asked me if I would like to make a date again and said, 'Will you meet me at the Queens Hotel in Manchester?' Back then the name of our rendezvous had no significance. A lifetime later it seemed bizarrely prophetic and one of the string of strange coincidences which have marked my whole life. It was a couple of bus rides away but I agreed. He said, 'You won't forget, will you'. Then he added, 'I'll make sure you don't forget,' and got an old white fiver out of his pocket and wrote the time and the date on it and gave it to me. And perhaps that's what made me turn up because selfishly I thought, 'He's got a few bob. He'll be able to buy me things.'

I certainly didn't think he was the kind of man who was going to take advantage of me. He had a very nice smile. I decided to go. I got the bus and I was walking up to the Queens and I got another shock. I saw this massive big American car with big yellow wheels. Rudi pressed the horn and it played a tune. I learned later it was a Chrysler Crown Imperial. Can you imagine the looks that attracted? This was 1965. I thought 'Jesus Christ, this man must be a billionaire'. I think I'd only ever been in a couple of taxis. I'd never been in a private car in my life. Nobody I knew in those days actually owned a car. This one was amazing - it had a little record player in it. It was Frank Sinatra singing *You Make Me Feel So Young*.

Rudi was shy and very quiet at first when he took me out on our first date, a meal at a restaurant way out into the country. He took me to this place far away from Manchester. I thought, 'I bet he brings them all up here'. I was excited and it seemed incredibly posh to me because the waitresses had aprons and the tables has lovely white tablecloths on. I felt nervous because here I was in the middle of nowhere with a man 20 years older than me. 'What if he leaves me up here? How am I going to get back?' I thought. Then I really started to panic. What if he just abandons me when I haven't got a penny in my purse. But he was just so nice. I didn't know he was hungry. Italians like to eat. He was ordering and trying to be a bit posh. I thought he was so mature and elegant with his car and his lovely clothes and his good manners and everything. It was like being with a prince. He ordered prawn cocktail followed by steak, which was the thing to have in those days, so I copied him and the waitress said, 'Would you like French fries?' He said, 'Yes please, and can we have some chips as well?' I might have been a bit wet behind the ears but I knew French fries were the same thing as chips. So all of a sudden I realised he wasn't quite as sophisticated as he made out, and I kept it to myself and started to relax a little. I noticed he had white stuff round his mouth and he kept swallowing little pills. I didn't know what to think and I wondered if he was taking drugs. I said, 'What are those?' He said, 'Rennies.' He said he suffered from terrible heartburn.

That broke the ice a little and we decided to drive back into town. He took me to a club full of loads of musicians who had finished work for the night. It was great. People came in and played for nothing and the atmosphere was wonderful. We stayed way past the early hours of the morning. I think it was seven or eight o'clock in the morning. Then I said, 'You can't take me home in the car. I'm not having any of my neighbours seeing me get out of that car.'

I decided to get the bus. I was running across Piccadilly to get the bus in my high hair, gold coat, tight skirt and black stockings. It was so crowded and I was rushing and I bumped into my Uncle Lawrence, of all people! He said, 'What are you doing? Where are you going?' I said, 'Oh I've had to do a late shift at the Cabaret Club and I've only just got off'. Somehow he believed me and I got out of it.

Rudi never touched me at all that first night. But it was still quite wonderful. And in those days communication was so much more difficult than today. We didn't have a telephone in the house so Rudi sent me a telegram to our house at Barmouth Street. He knew my husband wouldn't see it because he was out at work. So for our second date we agreed to meet at the Queens Hotel in Manchester and I got in his car again and he took me to another place and into another pub and we just had drinks there. At the time I used to drink brandy and coke. I really was never much of a drinker and I always filled up my glass with coke to take away the taste of the brandy. He was on gin and tonics and suggested I try one. I'd never had a gin and tonic in my life and I agreed to have one. I loved the taste and had another, and another. They didn't taste very strong but how much did I know? Before I knew it I had got so drunk he had to take me home in his car. It was dark by then fortunately, and he dropped me on the corner near our house. I was so drunk I don't know how I got into our house but I was ill for two days after that and I've never touched gin and tonic since. My husband went crazy. 'Where've you been?' he kept yelling and somehow I managed to convince him I'd got drunk at the Cabaret Club after work with the other girls.

Rudi and I went out a couple more times and soon I knew I had fallen for him in a big way. He felt exactly the same. The age difference didn't matter. We both knew we were in love and we soon started doing what lovers do. It was not like anything I had ever experienced before. It was wonderful, absolutely out of this world. I suppose we first had sex about two or three weeks after we first went out. He knew I was married and I knew he was married. But the attraction between us just grew. The key thing that drew me to him was the attention he paid to me. After a few meetings and getting to know him more, I really wanted him. He was giving me another life that I had never had before. I used to be sneaking out pretending I was going to work at night only I would meet Rudi on Ashton New Road near the New Royal; that was our meeting place, at two o'clock in the morning and then we would stay out all night.

Soon afterwards Rudi asked me to give up my job in the Cabaret Club. He didn't like me going in there with all those other men around. Never mind the fact I was married to someone else. He gave me the money instead and said it was just so he could see me every night and I could pretend I was going to work. He was certainly not paying for any sexual favours. He simply wanted to see me and he did not want me to work in the club. He would give me money so I could pretend to my husband I had been at work when I was really seeing him. And that is what we did. When I was staying in, instead of sending me flowers he used to meet me round the corner from my house and give me food. He used to bring me boxes of food. I used to come home with lovely steaks and things he had got from Yates's. We found ourselves dining on T-bone steaks in the middle of the week and my husband was astonished. I told my husband all sorts of rubbish and even pretended there was a woman at work whose husband worked in a butcher's. 'She nicks all this stuff and we buy it cheap,' I said. I was so much in love with Rudi I would have said anything, just to be able to keep seeing him.

I was quite happy to stop working at the Cabaret Club because Rudi did not like me going there. I just could not resist Rudi because he offered me the one thing I wanted in my life at that time which was total protection. At home I was in charge of everything in the house. I was in charge of kids, in charge of debts, in charge of all the money, in charge of what we ate and what we did. Every decision there was to take I took it. My husband was hardly ever there and when he was there he wasn't sober or he was rushing off to work in the morning.

Somebody now had put his arm round me and taken away all this worry and it made a huge impression on me. I was very unhappy at home but I still was not really quite prepared for this full blown affair. I was simply swept away by my emotions. Rudi had a wonderful personality. I liked everything about him but there was something about his wonderful combination of kindness and shyness that I found irresistible. He also had a wonderful sense of humour and he always made me laugh but his two most striking characteristics were kindness and shyness. I know he was 20 years older than me and I know he looked his age with his bald head. But his age never bothered me and I always thought he was handsome. You don't bother about a lack of hair when you're falling in love. I never did anyway. Certainly my husband was good looking and I had loved him at the start, but all the drinking had taken that love away.

You have got to have chemistry and Rudi and I had that. I'm not talking about the instant passion that produces a shag down an alley and nothing else. I'm talking about real, heart-stopping love that hits you so hard that you can't resist it, no matter how hard you try. It didn't happen straight away for me and Rudi, in fact it took weeks, perhaps months for it to fully overwhelm me. But that was months of getting to know each other, months of thoughtfulness and generosity, months of humour and irrepressible giggling because we always made each other laugh. Rudi was just more life enhancing than any other person I've ever known. In a few months, three or four probably, I was bowled totally over. And don't forget it was the sex as well. The sex, when it came along on the third or fourth time we went out, was entirely different from anything I had experienced with my husband. I had got married very early. I had only ever made love with one man. At the time it had seemed perfectly satisfactory. Me and my husband had a pretty normal love life, considering one of us was pissed a lot of the time.

Nowadays there are so many books, magazine articles and TV programmes telling you everything you could ever want to know about sex and plenty you don't. But when I was young there was hardly any of that. You and your lover just muddled through and worked it out for yourselves. With me and my husband it was just 'crash, bang, wallop'. But making love with Rudi was like nothing else I had ever felt before. It was exciting, fulfilling, demanding, surprising and hilarious and so, so satisfying. It was nothing like 'crash, bang, wallop'. I was in seventh heaven. He made me really happy in that department and I've every reason to believe that the feeling was reciprocated. I believe that there is an ideal man for every woman and as soon as I got to know him I knew that Rudi Mancini was mine. He was a wonderful man. Typically Italian, he loved food, music, passion and life itself. His father came over here in 1914. He ran away with a married woman from their little village and he could never go back home again, so perhaps it all ran in the family.

I am not proud to admit that from then onwards I launched into a life of total deception. Rudi became more important to me than life itself so we did what we could to be together as much as we could. Even if Rudi hadn't come along I don't believe my marriage would have lasted. I had lost the feelings I once had for my husband as I sat in alone and put the kids to bed alone and watched his dinner congeal in front of me alone. And once I saw at the Cabaret Club that there was more to life than a daily domestic grind of a two-up two-down existence with a drunken husband then I think if it had not been Rudi it would have been someone else. I definitely would not have stayed with my husband whatever had happened. I realised I had never been in love before. I thought I was in love at 15 with Raymond Massey, and I thought I was in love with my husband when I married him. But after I fell for Rudi I knew that I was wrong both times.

Rudi was very resourceful. He got a little flat down in Rusholme for us to meet and be together in. Sometimes it felt like playing house and we would just go to the flat and do ordinary things and be together and I think that was when I really fell completely in love with him. Sometimes I did think, 'What am I doing with this man? He's 20 years older than me,' but as soon as I was with him the question disappeared. Rudi was so kind to me. It was the kindness and the love-making that was second to none. And when I couldn't see him I just felt so sad.

But the longer Rudi and I carried on the affair the harder it became. His wife knew he was up to something so she used to get people to follow him and she found out that he was seeing me. We used to put money in the gas meter at our little flat to keep the place warm. And Rudi was always very careful with money even though he was always very generous with me. He noticed that the money he had put in the gas meter had run out much too quickly and it really puzzled him. Then one day when we were in bed together in the flat there was a loud bang on the door. It was his wife and she was screaming, 'I know you're in there. I know you're in there'. She had found out our hideaway. We learned later that she had had us followed to the flat and later gone to the landlord, who had never seen me. She insisted she was Mr Mancini's wife, which was true enough, and had forgotten her key. So she had been in waiting for us and used gas to keep warm while she was waiting. Only she missed us and then after that she sat there day after day waiting for us to come in. No wonder the money in the meter ran out!

But finally she came back another day and caught us, only Rudi always put the latch on the door so although she had a key she still could not get in. She yelled angrily outside for a while but eventually Rudi shouted at her and sent her away. After that she often used to follow us. Rudi was already having a bad time through our affair. He was out all the time. He would do what he had to do at the pub and then he would go off with me and he would be away from home all day. This mad passionate affair was absolutely crazy. We were both married to other people but we couldn't live without each other.

His wife found out who I was. I don't know how she got to know, but she did. I got home from work one day and my husband looked very grave and angry and he said, 'I've had a visitor at work today.' I knew this was serious. Scaffolding erectors don't have visitors at work who bring good news. Rudi's wife was canny the way she found him, because scaffolders work in different places every day. She had paid these lads from the pub to find out who I was and she told my husband that she was Veronica Mancini. I said, 'Who?' He said, 'She says you are going out with her husband'. I said, 'Me! Who is he?' He said, 'You know, that man that has the pubs in town.' I said, 'I don't know him. She's made a mistake.' He said, 'She says you've been followed and been seen with him. That's why she came to me. Why else would she come to me?'

I had to think fast but I've always been good at that. I said, 'Perhaps he goes in the club where I work. Take no notice.' I just denied, denied, denied and lied, lied, lied. He said that Mrs Mancini had given him a tenner. He said she had paid him to ring her and tell her the next time I went out. I just blustered it out. I said, 'Well, the only place I am going is to work and if she wants to follow me to work she is welcome to do it if she has nothing better to do with her time.' I think I convinced my husband that it was all the fantasy of an angry woman and he even gave me the tenner. So I went out and bought a frock from C & A. He was a good husband. He was always a good husband and he really loved me. But he loved drinking even more and it was too late for us to try again. I was besotted with Rudi and I would do anything to keep him. I was absolutely madly in love with him.

I am not proud of the way I behaved to my husband and my children but I just could not resist Rudi. If I could just be with him to laugh and love and live a little then nothing else mattered. It went on for two years. We went to Blackpool for a day, we had other flats, more lies, more rows at home; it went on and on. We didn't see each other every day by any means, like most loving couples. It was usually once or twice a week but we packed as much passion as possible into those meetings.

After two years I became really desperate. I thought I am going to leave my husband. I was desperate to get away and have a life with Rudi no matter what. I had a big row with my husband. It came out that he knew all about the affair. He said he had been told by lots of people, not just Rudi's wife, that I was with Rudi when I went missing. I had a plastic bag and I just stuffed make-up and stuff in it and I walked out. I went down town looking for Rudi. I didn't go in the club, I waited outside and spoke to one of the gay lads. He told Rudi I was outside and when he came out of the club I told him what happened.

He said, 'You'll have to wait until we finish.' I didn't know what to do, I was in complete despair. I remember standing with this pathetic bag of possessions near Smithfield Market crying my eyes out. I thought 'What am I doing here? What am I doing here?' He came out and got into this little box car he had and drove past with his wife and he didn't even look at me. They both knew it was me as I stood there in the light. Then he stopped the car a little way down the road and he came back to me. I was sobbing. I felt so sorry for myself and Rudi came up to me and said that his wife had just said, 'Bring her home!' He had told her that I had walked out on her husband and had nowhere to go. I didn't know what to do but I couldn't go to his house with her there so I went back home. Later she asked me to go and live with them in

Hill Lane, Blakely, where they had a big house. I said 'No'. I suppose it was very big-hearted and generous of her in a way but I couldn't accept. I just felt totally numb and deflated and I trudged off sadly and got the bus back home. And after that I didn't see Rudi for ages. Well at least a couple of weeks.

It was still awful at home and I still loved Rudi so nothing had really changed. I kept getting telegrams asking me to meet Rudi and when we met again he still felt the same way. We had these fleeting meetings because he was desperate to placate his wife and keep it secret. It just went on like that, seeing him only very occasionally and being lonely and miserable the rest of the time.

I was staying out that much that my mum was often left looking after the kids. My husband did try to look after the kids himself but everything went to pot. We lost the house because we got behind with the mortgage. It was all my fault my husband wasn't going out to work. I wasn't there, so often he couldn't go to work because he was looking after the kids. We did all these things just to be together. I became very depressed and most of the time I used to walk around crying. I knew it was my fault and that I was hurting people close to me but I just could not live without Rudi. I wasn't working any longer so we were really hard up. At home it was just one explosion after another. My husband and I had so many rows it seemed like a permanent war at home. He said, 'We're moving'. We couldn't sell the house so we just left it and got a house in Stanley Street, Salford, just round the corner from Coronation Street, which gave its name to the popular TV series.

My husband and I did try to rebuild our married life but if I'm honest my heart was never in it and it still wasn't working. It was awful because I just wanted to be with Rudi all the time. I still used to go out and stay an odd night with Rudi, I couldn't think of anything else. But Rudi's wife Veronica was determined to hang on to him. She even recruited Rudi's 17-year-old son to try to split us up. Rudi's son, a big lad called

Raymond, got in touch and said his dad urgently wanted to meet me at the club. I went to the club, because I was still going in on and off when she wasn't around. Raymond said his dad had been delayed and had to go somewhere and I was just to wait for him. I waited and waited and he never came. Raymond kept making excuses until the early hours of the morning. He had this house next door to his grandmother and said I could wait for Rudi in there.

I waited until it got to about eight o'clock in the morning and I'd had enough. I said, 'I'm not staying any longer, Raymond. This is ridiculous.' I got a taxi home. The next night Rudi used his other method of getting in touch - driving up and down and hooting a certain way and if I was in and heard it I would just say, 'I'm going to the shop,' and go out and meet him. He was really angry and he said he was never going to see me again. I said 'Why on earth not?' He said, 'You slept with our Raymond last night!' I couldn't believe my ears. I said, 'I didn't.'

Raymond was eight years younger than me and, in spite of his size, he was only a boy. The very idea was ridiculous. Rudi said that one of Veronica's best friends said that she had seen me coming out of Raymond's house at eight o'clock that morning. All of a sudden it started to fall into place. I explained to my angry lover that I'd been told he wanted to meet me. I had believed his own son, but now I realised it had been a plot to incriminate me. I was furious and shocked. I was devastated that Rudi was going to finish with me for something I hadn't done and would never do. Frantically I thought of ways to prove my innocence. I said, 'Ask Raymond what colour knickers I had on. Ask him about the mole on my back. Ask him anything. It's not true,' I pleaded hysterically. I said, 'Go back and ask him. I waited and waited for you and I was tired and you never came.'

In the end he realised I was telling the truth. I was bitterly angry with Veronica that she would stoop to doing something so devious and evil but with the passage of lots of years I sort of understand that desperate people do desperate things. At the time I just thought she was Mrs Wicked, but now I can even see it all from her point of view and I realise Mrs Wicked was only trying to keep a home together and I'm sorry for all the hurt I caused. Later I came to understand the agonies I put her through. I learned she battled with depression as she fought to keep her husband and I am truly sorry for that. I really am.

If anything it brought Rudi and I closer together. People who knew us said it was all because I had lost my father and I wanted a father figure. Not at all, I wouldn't have slept with my father, would I? To me Rudi was never a father figure. He was the man I loved to distraction, the man I couldn't live without. I knew it was wrong because I was married but it didn't feel wrong. When I was with Rudi everything felt wonderful. When we were apart I felt as if part of me was missing.

6

Blackpool

With two families torn apart by our affair I knew we couldn't go on as we were but we never planned our escape from the misery in Manchester. I know it sounds ridiculous, but it just sort of happened. One day I met Rudi and he said, 'I'm going to Blackpool next week for a day, would you like to come with us?' He wanted to go up to Blackpool with a friend of his called Tich Kite who was going to the seaside to see a lady friend of his called Madge and wanted us to go with him.

I never thought twice. I love Blackpool. I always have since I was first taken there as a child. Like many people from the north of England I always found the great bustling seaside resort had a certain magical quality. Anything could happen in Blackpool because while you're there real life back home was forever on hold. I thought it was a special place when I first visited as a child and it has never let me down since. And the chance to be with Rudi well away from everyone was just too good to resist. I just said 'Yes' straight away and I left with nothing but the clothes I stood up in. We got there and went out for the day with Tich and Madge.

We had a great day out and Madge said at night-time, 'You don't have to go home'. She had a flat where she said we could stay. It was 12 Garden Terrace, Blackpool, but it was not nearly as nice as it sounded. She said, 'You can stay in the basement flat.' We stayed a night and went out again the next night. And then we stayed another night. The basement flat was dark and damp and it had snails living in it. But to us it was a haven from the outside world. We ignored the snails and the dismal living conditions because at last we felt we were a real couple. The flat was a squalid dump but I've never been happier. We just shut ourselves off from the rest of the world. Our families, our partners, our previous lives were all completely blotted out for a while as we got on with the business of earning a living and expressing our deep, deep love for each other. It was very, very selfish, I admit.

Of course it is unforgivable for a mother to abandon her children. I know that, but I did it because I felt I had no alternative. I knew my mum and my husband and his mother between them would look after them so they were safe and well cared for. My husband might have drunk too much but he was a good father to our children.

I think we both realised at the same time that this was our big chance. No-one knew we were in Blackpool and no-one in Blackpool knew us. This was an opportunity for a fabulous fresh start. We hadn't planned a thing. Rudi had £80 on him, which was quite a bit of cash in the 60s but it was hardly enough to build a new life on. We never went home for three days, four days. We didn't know what to do. And then, in that grim basement flat, Rudi said to me, 'I'll look for a job playing the organ and you look for a job as a hairdresser or whatever. If we get jobs we'll stay and that's it.' I was thrilled and terrified at the same time. But Rudi said to me, 'We can never go back. We will make a go of our new life together.'

He got a job in a pub called the White Lion, where Yates's is today, playing the organ for £2.50 a session. It was May, 1967. I went for a job in the bar at the Queens Hotel that paid £8.50 a week and I got it. It was called the Tudor Bar then. All of a sudden we had a new life together. It was mad but it was wonderful. The best thing about it was that nobody knew where we were. We were blissfully happy and we were frantic to keep it a secret. We didn't tell anybody where we were. We were frightened the dream would end if we were discovered.

People ask me if I was happy. If you're shagging ten times a day you're going to be happy, aren't you? That's how happy we were. The truth of my life, and I'm not particularly proud of it in some ways, is that I just could not exist without the man I loved. I'm sorry that people got hurt on the way. We didn't want to hurt people but we did, both his family and mine. Rudi had a lot more to give up than I did. He had five children - Raymond, Alan, Rudi, Angela and Victoria - a wife and a thriving pub and nightclub business back in Manchester. He gave all that up for me.

At lunch times we used to go and have fish and chips on the sand and he used to meet me at the great big old back door of the Queens. It's still there and it looks just like a church door. We used to go and eat fish and chips on the beach and listen to Radio Caroline together. The flat was still awful but we were determined to make a go of it. It was very difficult because in those days it was really frowned on, a young woman running off with an older man. All his friends told him, 'Oh, it will never last, you know. She'll dump you when you get older.' And that did worry him. But I always knew it would last. I had to keep convincing him it was for life, our relationship. I had never been surer of anything in my life and I was right.

Rudi always had a very good business mind and he was thinking all the time he was working. I got this job as a barmaid. For weeks nobody knew where we were. I had left two kids and it was heartbreaking but I couldn't bring them. I just had to be with Rudi. It was just this draw we had for each other. We couldn't resist it. When I think back it still plays on my mind even now. Was I cruel? They were safe but I deserted them and the guilt will be with me until the day I die.

We were happy to stay in that first grotty flat with all the snails. Madge was very generous and she always seemed to have plenty of money. I learned soon after we arrived that she worked as a prostitute. I was not shocked, I already knew she was a kind and generous person so it didn't matter to me how she earned her living. She was fun. I was fascinated by the way she took great care getting ready to go out to work. She helped us such a lot that the mere fact that she was a prostitute made no difference to us at all.

Veronica never ever got married again or, as far as I know, never went with another man after Rudi left. She was madly in love with him and even though she was a very attractive woman she never wanted anyone else. She could have had other men but she thought he would go back to her. She always believed she would have him in the end but she was wrong, I'm afraid.

We worked really hard. We were determined to make it and I think our love drove us on. In this scruffy flat the telephone was going at all hours of the day or night. Madge said, 'Don't answer the phone. Don't answer the phone.' She didn't need to worry, I knew all the calls were from punters. Madge lived upstairs and the place was like a little boarding house with seven rooms and this awful basement flat. Madge was very canny, she let all the rooms out. It soon dawned on me that Madge had a heart of gold. If all the people she lent money to in Blackpool were lined up in the street it would be a very long queue. She's dead now but she was a one-off. She even used to leave 30 bob out for the burglars. She used to say, 'I always leave money out for them to find easily because then they don't smash the house up looking!' I'm not sure it worked but that was always her advice.

Of course no-one stays missing for long, particularly if they're earning a living as an entertainer in Blackpool. Rudi's sister found out where we were by chance. She was on holiday and walking past the White Lion one day when to her astonishment she heard Rudi playing. In those days he used to play his organ in the windows upstairs and the sound drifted out. When she heard it she said straight away to her husband, 'There is only one person who plays the organ like that, Rudi Mancini.' So they went in and there he was. They knew we were in Blackpool but they still didn't know where we were living.

Rudi and I were hard up, uncomfortable but blissfully happy until the day our cosy romantic world fell in. The worst thing that ever happened to me occurred on August 28, 1967. I will never forget the date. We were both working. I got a 'phone call in the Tudor Bar from my boss, the manager of the Queens Hotel, Mr Turner. He was a nice man, and he said gently, 'Pat you have to go home. Your husband is waiting for you'.

I was totally confused. To me, home was in Manchester, but I wasn't going back to my husband. I thought they had found us and my real husband had come to get me. So I rushed back to Rudi. As I got near the traffic lights I could see Rudi and I knew from the look on his face that something was tragically wrong. His eyes were full of tears and he was openly sobbing in the street. I knew it was the children. Something had happened to them and I knew this was my punishment for running out on them. As I got closer I said, 'It's the kids, isn't it?'

He couldn't answer me. I dragged on his coat and said, 'What is it? Tell me what has happened.'

His eyes were welling up with tears and I just said, 'Which one?'

He couldn't tell me. He just couldn't speak either. We got into the Garden Terrace flat and there was Madge and a policeman. 'Tell me, tell me,' I kept saying. 'Which one?'

The policeman just said, 'Boys will be boys.'

Madge spelled out the awful news to me - my son Dean had drowned.

I just screamed and went berserk. I pulled everything off the walls and went running around like a mad woman. It was horrendous. I was beyond grief, I was plunged into total despair and overwhelming guilt. This was my payback for leaving my children. The guilt is still there to this day. People ask me would you have your life over again and I have to say yes, but I'm not sure. Losing a child is a terrible thing and it's a terrible question and the answer should be no, because perhaps then I would still have my son today. I have punished myself over the years.

I had to get in a car and go back. Madge took me back. She drove me over with one of her boyfriends. I had to tell her not to come in because it was the first time I had seen my husband since I ran out on him. Rudi couldn't come with me. Feelings were running so high they would have killed him.

I went back to our terraced house to be confronted by my devastated husband. Grandma was looking after our daughter Pamela. It was the school holidays and my husband was off with them. They had been playing out. All these kids were playing by the canal and Dean fell in. If I had been at home perhaps it would not have happened so my life was suddenly filled with 'if onlys'. The hospital took over. I wanted to see my son but they put me in hospital and put me to sleep.

We got through the funeral somehow but I wouldn't go back to the house. The day after the burial I went to my mother's and Pamela was there. I went back to the cemetery where Dean was buried. The doctor had given me some sleeping tablets and I just took them all. I fell on the grave. One of the gravediggers found me lying on all the flowers and called an ambulance. I didn't wake up for three days. Eventually they brought me round and put me in Hope Hospital in Manchester, in a psychiatric ward. And all I wanted to do was be in a grave with Dean, because of the guilt. Harry's Auntie Edie was one of my visitors and she just kept saying to me. 'It's not your time to go.'

My husband was coming to see me and Rudi was writing me letters, asking if I wanted him to come back to be with me. He had left four children and a wife and a business behind when he ran off with me, leaving them a pub and a club and a house. His wife wanted him back, they had all been looking for us. He didn't know what to do because he didn't know if I was going to come back to Blackpool. He was living in a grubby flat on his own. He considered going back home to his wife, I know he did. She still wanted him back in spite of everything.

Rudi and I used to write little letters to each other. Also I had started to befriend my husband a bit. Things got a little better between us, but I just did not want to live any more. I was in such a suicidal state that I asked my husband to bring me in some make-up because I knew there were some razor blades I used to shave my eyebrows in my make-up bag. I went into the toilet and quite deliberately slashed my wrists. I just wanted to die, to be with my little boy.

It seemed the only way out of this awful pain. But they found me in time and stopped me. The marks are still there. They put me in another ward, where they could keep more of a watch over me. I knew I wasn't mental. They said my mind was disturbed and probably it was, but I knew why I wanted to do it. I just wanted to be with my son. Rudi was still writing to me so I thought I must go back to Blackpool to be with him. I wasn't allowed out of the psychiatric ward. I had a coat there, a nightdress and slippers. I'd been in there for three weeks. I had a few shillings that my mum had given me for papers. So I waited for a quiet moment, put my coat on over my nightdress and slipped out. But I knew they would miss me. I couldn't walk out down the driveway because I knew I would be seen so I hid in the bushes while they came out to look for me. I watched them rushing around looking and waited until they'd gone. When I thought it was safe, I walked out and got a bus to town and another bus to Blackpool. I was very weak but I was determined to make it, even though I was in my coat and bedroom slippers and nightdress. Rudi was waiting for me. I was still in a terrible state. I still just wanted to be with my son.

I was back with my beloved Rudi but my agony was far from over. The doctors wanted to put me in a mental hospital and they suggested electric shock treatment - it makes you forget, they said. I thought 'Great, I'll be better when it's over.' I didn't want to kill myself by this time. Rudi had got me feeling a bit better. But the treatment was horrendous. I woke up afterwards and looked at Rudi and said, 'Has Dean died?' And of course he had. I went back to doctor and complained. 'Oh,' he said, 'You have to have a few treatments.' I thought it would block it out, I felt so bad, but of course it never did. Nothing ever can.

7

Picking Up The Pieces

I didn't go back to work at the Queens. I just couldn't. I was hardly functioning. I still loved Rudi but I had all this grief and guilt over Dean and I was no use to anyone. Most of the time I wanted to simply crawl away and go to sleep and never wake up. But life has this astonishing habit of just going on and Rudi was like a rock.

In those early days together Rudi was always afraid I would leave him. He had given up so much for me and now he was reduced to desperate measures to earn a living. When he wasn't playing his music he would do anything to keep a roof over our heads. He even tried selling teddy bears along the beach and from door to door. He had to bang on doors with these big teddy bears and then ask, 'Do you want one of these for a shilling a week?' The finance company he was working for just wanted to get the customers hooked into credit and Rudi kept the money for the bears. He was a fine musician and a proud man and I knew it was a huge come down for him. We found out a lot about each other in those difficult first days together as a proper couple. The love was always strong but the trust built as well and we realised we were both grafters. No-one could beat us if we stuck together and the love grew stronger and stronger. If they had known back in Manchester that this man who was famous for his pub and his club and his big flash American car was selling teddy bears from door to door to earn a crust, they would have been shocked.

Even then £2.50 a session was low pay for a musician as talented as Rudi. But he wasn't well known in Blackpool like he was in Manchester. We thought that money we made would last for ever but when the end of the season arrived we got a shock. We had only ever been to Blackpool in the summer with the sun shining and thousands of people all over the place enjoying themselves. But in October the place was suddenly deserted and Rudi was out of work. He got another job on Central Drive in a little pub called the George that was a favourite with all the travellers. Blackpool is full of wonderful characters and we made friends with many of them, including people like gypsy Johnny Gallamore who still takes holidaymakers for rides along the front. There was a lot of local trade and Rudi filled the place winter and summer. He left there to go to a better job in the Victory on Corn Street. That was a big pub and eventually he was to fill it up winter and summer there. So he was starting to build up a whole new following with his music because he was a brilliant musician.

After a while Madge said, 'I'm moving to Hodder Avenue. Do you want to come with me? You can have a bedroom there.' It seemed ideal, until we were raided by the police. Rudi and I were out at the time so we were not involved. Madge tried to say she was not on the game, she just liked to bring boyfriends back. But the police wanted to know why she had four dozen Durex in the house. Madge said she had a lot of boyfriends.

We thought it might be time to move on. What were we going to do, I wondered. Rudi said, 'Do you fancy running one of these little guest houses?' His business mind took over. Rudi's mother Clementina had always told him that boarding houses were a good business. Model lodging houses, she called them. I wasn't so sure. I was only 28 at the time and boarding house landladies always seemed to be middle-aged at least.

But we went looking for a new business and first we found a boarding house in Yorkshire Street that we liked and we put down a £200 deposit. It seemed fine but soon afterwards we saw one that was a much better prospect, a little boarding house called Arden House in St Bede's Avenue in Blackpool. The valuation was £1,100 to take it over and then, of course, there was £5 a week rent to pay.

We desperately wanted to switch to St Bede's but we risked losing our deposit on the other one. We wanted to get out of it so I found out from the estate agent that the property was owned by an old lady. I made out it might be somebody I knew and he told me the name. I found it in the telephone book and I rang her up. I didn't tell her who I was and just said I had wanted to put in an offer on Yorkshire Street but the estate agent reckoned someone had beaten me to it. She sounded sympathetic and I knew she was an old woman who probably was a little old-fashioned in some of her ideas and attitudes. So I said I felt let down to be pipped at the post by an Italian. 'Really,' she said. Clearly the estate agent had not passed Rudi's name on to her. I said that I desperately wanted that place and I felt upset to be beaten to it by someone not from this country, someone who was Italian! The next day the estate agent rang us up and said he was returning our deposit and he admitted the owner didn't want 'foreigners' in her place.

Rudi and I had a good laugh at that afterwards as we learned that sometimes prejudice can even work in your favour. It was a bit devious but £200 was a lot of money in those days. I was starting to find a sense of purpose in my life for the first time in months.

So we went back to St Bede's Avenue and somehow got the money together. Madge, bless her, lent us £250 and we begged, borrowed and stole the rest. It was a struggle. This was in 1968 and by then Rudi's sister was in touch with us and she lent us another £250. We were so desperate we went to a loan firm but we were still £250 short and the fellow who wanted to get out lent us that and put us on a fiver a week!

There were seven bedrooms and regular customers booked in to arrive so there we were in the spring of 1968 with our brand new business. While student unrest and fear of revolution swept Europe we had more urgent and mundane problems facing us. Having exhausted every possible source of credit, we had not a penny between us and we had a family of six booked in to arrive on our first day of opening. I'll never ever forget that first day we opened. I was trembling with fear. I had never done anything like this before. I had to feed and cater for complete strangers and I was absolutely terrified. Rudi still had his playing job but we had already borrowed on his wages and we had no money to get the food.

Sylvia and Eric Brown, who came from Manchester, lived over the road and I thought perhaps I could try to borrow it from them or maybe Rudi would ask for a sub on his wages. But before I could do anything there was a knock on the door and when I opened it this woman said, 'Who are you?'

'I'm the new landlady,' I explained nervously.

'Where's Claire?' said my first guest and I realised I was 28, flat broke and looking anything but the jolly seaside landlady. I had no confidence in myself and I looked thin and drawn after everything I'd been through.

'Claire's sold it to us,' I explained weakly and she didn't look very impressed but she boomed at me, 'Well, we're the Walfords and we always pay upfront,' and handed me a load of money and marched in with her family.'

It was £8.50 a week to stay for full board and I could have kissed her. I ran out and bought six slices of beef, six slices of bacon and six eggs. We were so green that in the morning I broke an egg and Rudi ran out and bought another one. That's how clueless we were. We did the breakfast and cleared up. Then he went to work playing the organ. From that moment on it was pretty frantic because we had to do everything ourselves and Rudi was away playing the organ a lot. My life

*Our first boarding house, Arden House in St. Bede's Avenue, Blackpool.
Even the garden swing seat was rented out for £1 a night!*

The Mancini Hotel on Blackpool's Promenade, 1973

Signing the wedding register with Rudi
April 7th 1973

Rudi and me with Rudi's son, Raymond,
outside the Queens Hotel

Enjoying a glass of champagne aboard Concorde

*The Palm Court Hotel where we had six very successful years
before buying the Queens Hotel*

*The Gables in Lytham, the house Rudi and I bought in 1987
but only spent one night in before returning to our flat in the Queens*

Ready for the Captain's cocktail party aboard the QE2

Taking over the Queens Hotel in 1985

*Receiving the MBE at Buckingham Palace in 2006
with my brother Paul, daughter Pamela and sister Sharon*

*At the Queens with (left to right) Norman Collier, Johnny Casson, Roy
'Chubby' Brown, Pat Mancini, Jeremy Beadle, Frank 'Foo Foo' Lamar*

My son Dean, pictured just before he died, and his sister Pamela

My daughter Pamela (centre) with my grandaughters Adele (left) and Gemma

Pat Mancini MBE

became cooking and cleaning. Fortunately I knew how to. My mother had taught me everything she knew and we were taught housewifery at school. Working helped me put my life back together. I'd just work, work, work.

It was tough but at the end of our first season in the boarding house business we had made enough of a profit to join the traditional annual Blackpool exodus to Majorca. It cost £72 for a month in the sunshine, full board at a nice hotel and it was brilliant. All the Blackpool hoteliers and boarding house people went. We knew everybody there and we felt as if our life together was going to be happy. We had bad news from Manchester because we heard that Rudi's wife had lost the pub. The business had depended so much on Rudi's personality and skill as a musician that she really struggled after he left.

Rudi was upset but he couldn't go back. Our contact with our former partners had completely ceased by then. I tried to get to see Pamela but my husband stopped me. In those days I was still very naïve. I didn't know my rights. I had no idea about a mother's right of access to her children. And I was still gripped by the most awful guilt over what I had done to my family. I thought my husband was in the right to keep me away because I had walked out. I know now that was wrong, but it was what I thought at the time.

Once I did go back to Manchester and tried to pick Pamela up from school. I was at the gate and she saw me and screamed. She would not come with me. At night-time I went to my mother's and my husband came round and said I was never to go near her again. He was very angry and he threatened to hit Rudi. Well Rudi was a lot older than he was, so I was terrified he would hurt him. Harry and I were still married at that stage so I was so full of guilt over my affair and Dean's death that I somehow could not challenge my husband then. I just thought, 'I have done wrong by leaving so he is in the right by telling me to stay away'. I didn't think I was entitled to anything. Rudi comforted me and said, 'Don't worry. One day, when she is older, she will come to you.' Mercifully those gentle, well-meant words were later to come true.

Then Rudi saw a little hairdresser's shop in Grosvenor Street to rent; it was all fitted out. It was only a couple of hundred to go in and Rudi said, 'You could do that in the winter.' So I became a hairdresser again - anything to make a few bob. It was half a crown to have your hair washed, dried and set in the winter of 1969. It worked really well for a while; it was only a small shop and I was running it on my own and building up the business. But the problem came at Easter when the boarding house opened again. Suddenly I had to be in two places at once. We had to serve breakfast, lunch and dinner, so I used to get up early in the morning and do the breakfasts and then come back to the hairdressers where the customers would already be waiting. I would somehow have to get out of the hairdressers to get back to serve lunch. I prepared soup and salad early in the morning and then do a proper dinner at night. I used to finish early in the hairdressers to get back to do the dinner. It was just totally exhausting. I was dashing backwards and forwards from the shop to prepare meals for the guests. I worked myself into the ground. At the end of the season I knew I could never repeat it and we sold the hairdresser's. I think we got £300 for the lease and I was mightily relieved. That was a season I could never have repeated.

Then this amazing, mad-busy chip shop came up for sale round the corner. It was called Dawson's Fish and Chip Shop and it was a brilliant business because it was always packed. You could smell the place from miles away. I was amazed to realise it was the very same place that had got me into bother as a kid for eating fish and chips in the street but at least I knew it had a long history of success. Rudi and I thought it would be an absolute goldmine, you could never get served quickly because it was so busy. We decided that if we got this chip shop we'd be millionaires inside a year because it was so fantastic. We were about to learn another important business lesson: don't take on more than you can handle.

In those days we were so full of youth and enthusiasm we didn't care that we didn't really have enough money to run the business. That's when you find yourself learning pretty fast how to be enterprising. We would do almost anything to survive. Sometimes we pulled all sorts of dodges when people were fighting to get rooms. We've let a bathroom as a bedroom by just putting a board on a bath and a mattress of top. In the old days there were so many people in Blackpool and everybody wanted somewhere to sleep. When all the hotels were full the police used to ask private householders to take visitors in because they were concerned about people wandering the streets at night. We had a hammock outside and one night we let that for someone to sleep in!

We would do anything to make more money but the time we tried to divide a bedroom to double the income went badly wrong. A friend of Rudi's from the pub where he used to play reckoned he was a bit of a builder and did the job. Two of them came and they were at it all day but they must have been half cut because they split the room the wrong way so one half had all the windows and the other one was like the Black Hole of Calcutta! And we needed the rooms that weekend. I ended up putting a big picture of a sea scene on the wall so our guests had an idea of what they were missing. We let some people we knew have that room the first time to test it out. The guy was called Eric Grant and he was a big fan of Rudi's music and he and his wife Vera used to follow Rudi all over to hear him play. Eric's favourite number was *Tangerine*. He used to say, 'Play Tangerine'. Next morning he came down and said, 'Bleeding hell, Rudi. I woke up and I didn't know if it was night or day. There's not a glimmer of light in that room. I couldn't find the light switch and we thought we were going to be in there for the rest of our lives.' Later we had an elderly couple in there and she lost her teeth somewhere. It was so dark she never did find them. Needless to say we had to change everything and split that room the right way so both halves had a window.

A cowboy builder built us a lean-to toilet but he wasn't

exactly the most careful builder. Instead of building it on foundations he built it on big oil drums and the bleeding thing sunk! It was another dodgy job. There was a surprise drop when you went outside if you weren't careful. A singer friend of ours called Jackie Marshall came in this beautiful new white suit, looking so smart. He wanted to go to the toilet and went out the back and got covered in mud and grime. He was a real mess.

After a while my mum used to come up and help me, because she loved cooking. It was just horrendous some days, you wondered how you got through but somehow we did. But going through all that with Rudi, we both knew we could not fail. We had come through so much to get where we were. And we were still very much in love.

Still, with two different fledgling businesses to run and no proper capital behind us we had to resort to desperate measures to keep the show on the road. We called it 'dodging up' as we had to pull all sorts of strokes because we had no money to bring in proper craftsmen. When we were in the fish and chip shop we had part of a secondhand range put in and I installed it myself. We had no choice because it was £12 for the electricity people to come and we couldn't afford that. I didn't know how to do it so I found out and did it, and that range always worked perfectly. You had to make do and mend in those days - it was that or the business would go under.

We began the season full of optimism but we pretty soon got a reality shock. We were still doing all the meals at the boarding house and Rudi was going off playing the organ and I was left in the chip shop at night. We did that for a whole season and it was horrendous. Rudi was no good with his hands, apart from making wonderful music. So he was never that practical but he could decorate. In the winter we would go upstairs and decorate. It was all small rooms. Five rolls of wallpaper would do a room and we'd just emulsion the ceiling.

I used to go round to the chip shop in the middle of the night painting it all. I had all the lights on and I would be slapping emulsion all over the place and the local coppers used to call in for a cup of tea. I had to do things myself because we couldn't afford to pay anybody to come in. I thought I already knew what hard work was when I walked into that fish and chip shop but I had no idea. Being a total novice didn't help. I burned the fat more times than I can remember. I don't know how we got through that season. My mum even came over to help. It seems incredible but through all my traumas I hardly ever spoke to my mother about what was going on in my life. We just didn't in those days, you didn't tell your mum a thing. Now they come crying for everything but then it was different.

But even my hard-working mum couldn't rescue me. We had some real nightmares in that shop. Back then I used to have two poodles and she shut them in the kitchen under the table. I made the mistake of putting hot fat in a rubber bucket and suddenly we found the whole shop floor was covered in the stuff because it had melted its way through the bottom. The dogs were yelping in pain and sliding all over because their paws were in hot fat. My mother was a bit shocked by all the chaos.

There was just a mass of people who all seemed to arrive at once. We sold a lot of fish and chips but it was terribly hard doing it after you've already done a whole day's work. We had a coach party come in and they all wanted serving at once but we hadn't got enough fish so I cut all the fish in half. It was a total lack of experience. One night Rudi even ate a bad fish to prove to an awkward customer that it was perfectly all right and just on the turn. We thought we were making money but as it turned out we weren't. Halfway through the season British Railways closed down the station that brought us all our customers. The place changed overnight from being mad-busy to being a white elephant. All our customers disappeared. It was just dreadful.

We realised that the guy we bought the place from must have known the station was going to be shut down. It was a disaster, really. At the end of the season I just put the lid down on the fryer and leant on it and prayed, 'Please God don't let me ever have to open this again.' And he didn't. We sold the place a couple of weeks afterwards and that helped to give us enough money to buy a property and that's when we moved to a bigger boarding house on Dean Street.

We sold St Bede's Avenue for about £2000 - enough for the deposit on the boarding house in Dean Street, which had 14 bedrooms and much more potential. It was called the Dexter, but we didn't like that name and we changed it to the Fiesta after our wonderful first holiday in Majorca. It's still there today and the little bed and breakfast sign that a friend of ours put up is still there as well. Every time I pass an old place I get a little blast of nostalgia.

We opened the following week at Easter and some surprise help arrived in the shape of Neville St. Clair, a gay friend of Rudi's who turned up on the doorstep. That wasn't his real name of course, he was actually called Neville Ball, but as he was known as 'Neville Knacker' at Sunday School you can understand him changing it. He had been working in the Wakefield Theatre Club but evidently the drag act he performed was being phased out and suddenly he was short of a job and somewhere to live. We said there was room in the cellar but he would have to wash up. Neville only had the clothes he stood up in and £100. Rudi suggested he revived his drag act and sent him off to buy a frock and a wig and some make-up. At night-time he went up to the Victory and did his act with Rudi. All of a sudden he had a life; he stayed working with Rudi at nights and with us in the day time in various establishments for the next 34 years.

Pretty soon I learned never to be surprised by the behaviour of the great British public. In my experience most people are fine if you treat them properly but there are always strange exceptions. In this boarding house in Dean Street we had the woman whose husband died in the night. We were mortified and we expected her to be even more upset. Far from it, she was so unshaken by her sudden bereavement she tried to sell her dead husband's shirt the very next morning.

I remember one guest asking me up to his room and making me reach onto the top of the wardrobe. I did and I found it was covered in dust but I got the point. I didn't know you had to dust on the top of the wardrobe. I'd never had a wardrobe before. I was used to hanging my clothes on a nail on the back of the door where I'd come from, but that taught me a good lesson.

We always seemed to be frantically busy. It was work, work, work doing three meals a day and getting all the beds changed and ready. Rudi and I were sleeping in the basement by then because we couldn't afford to occupy a bed.

When we were in Dean Street a couple used to come and stay and ask us to come out with them. We were still working very hard and Rudi was playing at the Victory. He was always very tired when he came home. But this couple's daughter was a singer and they pestered me to go and see her perform at the North Shore Working Men's Club. I didn't want to go but I agreed and said, 'You go on and I'll follow you when I've cleared away'. I got a cab and was chatting away to the driver and said, 'I've got to go to the Club tonight to listen to some bloody boring singer. She's the daughter of one of the guests and I have to go because they are really good regular customers'. It was pretty awful as I'd feared. She was only a young girl just starting. On the way back the singer and her mum and dad all got in the cab with me and we had the same driver. As he pulled away, he turned to me and said, 'How was that boring singer?' My face went bright red and I felt so embarrassed. I tried to cover by saying, 'I was telling you about another singer altogether,' but I don't think I got away with it.

I was catering for 40 people. It was full board again and Rudi was still going out playing. It was terribly hard work and in 1970 I got pregnant when we were in there. I suppose it should have been wonderful news, but how could I have a baby? It was the worst possible time. My mother had dreadful problems of her own as my stepfather had been taken in to Christie's Hospital in Manchester desperately ill with cancer. Rudi and I wanted to go over and visit him to support my mum. We knew he was dying and, although it was hard to find time, we were frantic to go and see him. We left Neville to do all the high teas, having prepared all the soup and other stuff, and he had someone lined up to help him.

On the way there I began to miscarry. At first I thought I had wet myself, but I was bleeding. We had to turn back and call the doctor. He said I would have to go into hospital myself but that was just not possible. I said, 'I can't. I've got 40 people in here relying on me and I can't let them down.' He said he strongly advised me to go to hospital because I could haemorrhage at any moment. But if I refused to go to hospital, he advised me to stay in bed and rest. I couldn't do that either of course. He gave me some pills and I went on catering, only either Rudi or Neville had to physically pick me up from the settee and carry me to the stove so I could cook the breakfasts, the lunches and the dinners. We did that for about two weeks after this miscarriage. It was the only way we could get through it and it was one of the hardest things I have ever done. If you've got 40 people who have come to have a hard earned holiday staying with you, you simply can't be ill. We didn't have staff it was just us and if the business went down we stood to lose everything so I carried on.

I used to love to watch *Fawlty Towers* because I thought it was hilarious but everything that happened to John Cleese was exactly the sort of things that happened to us. Only it's not always so funny if you're on the wrong end of the awkward customer or the crisis in the kitchens.

If you look as if you have a bob or two people always ask you how to make money. My advice is that unless you happen to be a Lottery winner there is no substitute for simple hard work. We just never stopped. Rudi went out and played his music and worked in the hotel whenever he wasn't playing. I just worked in the hotel every waking hour I had. Looking back I suppose I must have been driven by what had happened to me. I was haunted by Dean's death for a long, long time and I know now that I will never get over it as long as I live. I think perhaps because of the way we got together it always seemed as if the whole world was against us. But we were very determined to make a success of our business. We learned by running the Fiesta, with its 14 bedrooms, that the only way to really succeed was to be bigger and better.

We had a few personal things to get sorted out as well. Rudi and I really wanted to become husband and wife and in 1970 we decided it was about time. We both needed to get divorced so we could get married. I got a lawyer and put in for my divorce. I had to go to Manchester and that was the first time I had seen my husband since I was lying ill in the hospital after Dean died. After we had been apart for two years there was really nothing he could do to stop the divorce going through.

We met in the courtroom and looked at each other bleakly and said nothing. He got custody of Pamela and I never fought that because I just still thought I was in the wrong because I had gone off and left the marriage. I thought it was automatic that the parent who had stayed got custody. Nobody ever said to me that I might have had rights as well. Then afterwards he walked away in one direction and Rudi and I walked away in another and it was all over. We came back to Blackpool and had a bit of a celebration.

Then it was Rudi's turn and again there was nothing his wife could do to stop the divorce because they had been separated for more than two years. But she asked for £600, which was a lot of money in those days, because she wanted to buy a pub. That was the price of our freedom. We managed to borrow the money and she agreed that was her final demand. Years later she tried to come back on us and ask for more money when she realised we were doing well but she didn't get any more because she had signed that agreement.

After we had run the Fiesta for three seasons, we knew we both liked the job. But in Blackpool, as in any seaside town, the only real place to be is on the Promenade. We were dying to get on the front. We kept looking for the right place and an estate agent contacted us with news that there was a woman with a place on the front she was keen to sell. Evidently her husband had sold his big haulage business and had put a big deposit down on another hotel and they needed to do a deal quickly.

As soon as we heard about the hotel we knew it was just what we wanted. It was on the front with 16 bedrooms, only two more than we had, but it was a much better location. The estate agent explained that this couple were desperate to sell because they risked losing their deposit on the other hotel they wanted to move to. In the end we did a complicated deal where they bought the place we were selling and I bought the place on the front and the lawyers did the job in double quick time for once. They say that it takes six weeks to complete, but we did it all in a fortnight. We had bought the Fiesta for £8,500 and we sold it for £18,000 as property prices were beginning to rise fast. It cost £25,000 to buy the new place, which was only a little bit bigger than the Fiesta but it had a bar and a lounge and most important of all it was on the front.

It was coming up to Easter 1973 and we were so enthusiastic about finally getting a place on the Promenade that perhaps we did not look at the hotel as closely as we should have done. We knew how desperately we wanted the hotel, which we already planned to call the Mancini, so we could really make our mark on Blackpool.

But we had some rather pressing personal arrangements to attend to at the same time. We got married on April 7 and it was Easter the following week. We had really wanted to get married on April 14, which was Rudi's birthday, or April 11, my birthday. But the only available date they had in the Registry office in Quay Street in Manchester was April 7, so that was that. We wanted to get married in Manchester because that was where all our friends were.

By then everyone from our fractured families and all our friends knew where we were and they were all back in touch. But only one of Rudi's sons, Raymond, came to the wedding. And that week I had to go for a licence to sell alcohol at the Mancini. I had never had one before. Rudi had, but he could not go for one this time because he had a conviction from his pub days in Manchester still hanging over his head.

Rudi's brush with the law happened in the early 1960s long before I met him, in the days when he used to put drag acts on in his pubs. They were very different times then. Swearing on stage was illegal and live entertainment was all very strictly regulated, but in spite of the restrictions Rudi was doing very well. But in 1962, he was summoned because of alleged blasphemy on stage. He was taken to court and his lawyer was a very bright and outspoken young lawyer called George Carmen who was just starting his career in Manchester at the time. The case made huge headlines in all the papers, particularly the *News of the World*. The police had used a very butch undercover policewoman who had been going in night after night watching and trying to get evidence to take Rudi to court. Neville used to sing the famous Peter Sellers' song that goes, '*Oh Doctor, I'm in trouble. Well, goodness gracious me... Boom boody-boom boody-boom boody-boom boody-boom-boom-boom…*'

The case went on for a long time and eventually when this butch policewoman got into the witness box George Carmen said to her, 'Right officer, show me how the song went.' She was very embarrassed but she had to do it, only her version made it 'Bum titty bum titty bum titty bum, bum, bum.' Carmen said 'Oh no officer. He sings it much faster than that. Could you give us the correct version, please'. She did it again and it just about brought the house down at the Law Courts. Carmen kept making her go faster and faster. The judge was struggling to keep a straight face and he admitted, 'I don't know whether that was a diddy or a titty… case dismissed.'

George Carmen absolutely ridiculed the policewoman and the police case. Afterwards he said to Rudi, 'Look, get out of that pub.' Rudi said, 'Why? We've won the case!' Carmen, who was a big drinker and became one of Rudi's best customers said, 'They'll have you. They know you've got away with one here and they will never let it lie. I've got you off, now get out before they come back and get you for something else.'

Rudi admitted to me years later that he ignored this advice because he was cocky. The pub was going well at the time. He had won the case. He became a little big-headed and thought no-one could touch him. Rudi always liked the police and he knew in our business it was important to always keep in with them. The following Christmas the police rang Rudi up one night and asked him to do them a favour. They had been let down for entertainment at a police function and asked if he could stand in at the last minute with his accordion and provide some music. He explained that he did not finish until 11pm and they said that would be fine, so he agreed. As soon as his own spot had finished he dashed out to his car and had moved it only a couple of yards when the police swooped. It turned out he had no insurance and they knew it. Back then it was an automatic prison sentence and he was given three months in prison. The police were so determined to get their revenge for being made to look foolish in court that they deliberately set him up. George Carmen said, 'I told you so'. And his mother dressed in black and sobbed outside Strangeways every day, pleading with the prison authorities to let her son out. When he went in, the other inmates all started cheering because everyone knew him in Strangeways.

So all these years later when we came to get a licence for our new hotel, he couldn't go up for it. Right, so there was nothing else for it. Still single just a few days before we were to get married, I went up in my own name of Patricia Talbot. And I was scared to death of attending in a court for a licence. I had never been inside one in my life. Rudi came with me in his brand new tweed car coat that was the latest thing in those days. The police had been round to inspect the place and they said they had no objections. We'd been really busy getting the place all ready. Then on the Wednesday just three days before the wedding I went into the court and the police officer stood up and objected.

I thought 'You bastard. You came round the other day and told me everything was all right'. He said, 'We have been investigating and discovered she is getting married on Saturday to Mr Mancini, who has run pubs in Manchester and has a conviction for allowing foul language on stage.' I sensed that Rudi expected trouble and did not fancy being hauled over the coals. He started to make a sharp exit and I just saw the back of this car coat disappearing out of the door leaving me to face the music alone. 'Thanks a lot, Rudi,' I thought. He was ashamed of his past being read out in court.

'Really,' said the magistrate. 'Who is this lady here? Miss Patricia Talbot or Mrs Rudi Mancini?' 'It is Patricia Talbot, sir, but she is getting married on Saturday to Mr Rudi Mancini.' But the magistrate was terrific. He said to this policeman, 'This is Patricia Talbot we're dealing with, who has no convictions, not Mrs Mancini. Objection overruled, I grant the licence to Patricia Talbot'. One moment I was a nervous wreck and the next I was just very relieved.

On the following Friday we went to Manchester and I stayed at my mother's house and Rudi stayed at his cousin's and we had the wedding in the morning at Jackson's Row Registry Office and it was a wonderful, wonderful experience. We had waited so long to become man and wife and we were both very happy. In fact we were in such a whirl that we completely forgot to get the car taxed. It sat, decked in ribbons, just outside the police station near the Registry Office but happily no-one noticed! There were about 100 people there to share it with us. We got married and then went back to my Auntie Kath and Uncle John's until the evening reception in the Thomson's Arms at the back of the Piccadilly Hotel, run by an ex-boxer. We had a drink in the Prince of Wales with a few of my uncles and friends and family and then later we came back into town for a lovely party. We had Shirley Bassey playing all the way through the meal and it was fantastic. We had a great, great time. We both went back to my mother's for our first night together as a married couple. There were no thoughts of a honeymoon because we had run out of money with the new business and the wedding. But I had a fabulous dress and a fabulous day and I think the bill for the whole thing was about £120. I danced and danced and I was so happy to see my family and his friends mixing and getting on so well. I thought, 'This is it. This is what we have been striving for all these years.' Raymond was the only one of Rudi's sons who came, as the others had still not forgiven their dad for walking out on their mother. When people asked what we wanted for wedding presents I just said, 'Pots, tea services, blankets, sheets and stuff we need for the new place.'

The Mancini felt like a huge step forward. It cost £25,000, which was a fortune at the time but it was worth every penny. We had a bar there and, thanks to the wisdom of the court, a licence to go with it. It made an enormous difference because we put an organ there so instead of Rudi going out to play he could play in our own place. He kept all the guests in with his fantastic music and he soon brought in a whole lot more customers from outside as well. But I was doing the food and then straight in the bar until three or four o'clock in the morning. Sometimes I was so busy I didn't have time to wash my feet for days. It was all work, work, work. There was no time to do anything else.

We were frantically painting one room at a time, desperately trying to get the whole hotel done before we opened. All the furniture was piled in one room to give us space and at night we just climbed on a pile of mattresses to snatch a bit of sleep. When we opened I think we had six guests booked in and by the end of the day that had gone up to 40 and we were full. At breakfast every table had a different tea service on it. All the blankets were different.

But it was all a panic. When I went to look in the kitchen I was horrified to find there was no proper catering oven, just an ordinary domestic one. We had been so busy with the licence and the wedding to even check the place properly. I didn't find out until the night before and I had to stay up nearly all night cooking all the chickens ready for the next day because I knew we'd have no time otherwise. That first week in there was horrendous. Some of the legs of the beds were broken and we discovered that an A-10 size catering tin was just the right height so quite a few of the beds were resting on tins! We took the labels off but we made a mark on the tins so we knew whether it was beans or peaches or whatever because we were certainly going to use them at some point. One woman came to me and said, 'We've had a great time here but I wish we'd had some cream.' I said 'What for?' She said, 'To eat the tin of peaches with'. Neville had left the bleeding label on!'

In those days lots of Scottish people came down. It took them five hours in those days to get down to Blackpool from north of the border, so they would leave late at night and arrive at Blackpool early in the morning and you had to get them all in the lounge and settle them down to try to catch up on a bit of their lost sleep because their beds still had people in them. We then had to do all the breakfasts for the guests before they left and get all the rooms ready for the Scottish people. It was a nightmare of work, absolutely horrendous. That was our Saturday when they were coming down to see the lights. And people would stay a fortnight in those days. They would often pay you the lot up front but then after a week they would announce, 'Our Elsie is coming tomorrow', or 'Our Maisie', or 'Our Arthur,' and we were expected to find somewhere for them to sleep. I would say, 'There's no more room,' and they'd say, 'Give us the sheets and we'll sort it out ourselves'. We never quite knew where they were in the house but they were sleeping with someone and they would pay you up front. They were fantastic customers and in spite of everything they say about the Scots, in my experience they are <u>not</u> tight. They used to leave saying, 'As long as we've got enough money for a loaf of bread, a bottle of milk and a quarter of tea we'll be all right'. They used to spend. The only problem was that they would have you in the bar until half past three of four o'clock in the morning. We had to be up to do the breakfasts for eight o'clock but half of them would not get up because they were still in bed.

8

Wanted And Unwanted Guests

The great thing about running a hotel is the people. Customers come in all shapes and sizes and they never fail to fascinate me. People are so unpredictable. We had a guest who sadly died and his son treated the tragedy as if his father had just been an ordinary person who he hardly knew. It was just as if it was another case to him. We were all scared, wondering how we were going to break the news. He was a very imposing man, a great big fellow, but he just took it as if it was part of his job. The father was not well and he had been taken on holiday in the hope it would improve his health. But it didn't. His son was just so flat and unemotional. I have never seen anybody so cold in my life. His own father was dead and he just said, 'Pack his things up and leave them there and we will get it sorted.' We found out later he was a serving policeman, a detective in fact, so maybe that helped to explain it.

I suppose I always had something to prove because a lot of people thought Rudi and I wouldn't last together. They said, 'She'll leave him when he gets a bit older'. He was successful in Manchester and I knew we could be successful in Blackpool but it was like us two against the whole world. I knew I would never leave him.

We had been in the Mancini quite a while when that delight of all small businesses, Value Added Tax, was introduced. I have never known how to do books properly. I just grab everything and give it all to the accountant. I always found VAT really complicated although they told me it was simple: you just had to move a dot, but I never knew in which direction.

It was winter when they sent someone round to make sure we were doing it right. I had phlebitis so I was hardly feeling my best and we sat there in front of this one bar electric fire in a room at the back of the bar. I had to keep the weight off my legs. I chatted him up and said I was only a cook who didn't understand figures and I was so pleased he had come to help me. He seemed a bit surprised and said, 'Not many people are pleased to see us.' He was very gentle with me and he slowly took me through it all. We became friends until, on the way out, he spotted a fruit machine. 'What's that?' he asked ominously. I had to explain and he was not amused that the income from the machine featured nowhere in our accounts. I blamed inexperience and I said it was just like putting money in the 'grid' in the road: 'Why should I have to tell you?' He smiled and said, 'Mrs Mancini, you're the grid! Starting from now, please include the figures.' I think I had charmed him a little by then. You have to know how to get round people in my business, especially the VAT man.

After the season ended we decided we had earned a holiday. I didn't like flying so we took the banana boat from Southampton to the Canary Islands. I imagined there'd be loads of bananas and flies but it wasn't quite like that. It cost £72 for five days to Las Palmas and back; we stayed a month and took Neville. On the boat he sang and Rudi played organ and they did a great show on board. I wore my flamboyant gold dress and coat and topped it off with tiara that I'd had for wedding. No one was going to ignore me! As we'd been hard up when we booked they put us in a cheap cabin near the engines. There were just small bunk beds and a tiny sink. We decided to celebrate one night and we all got very drunk. I woke up in my gold coat, still wearing my tiara and Rudi was nowhere to be seen. The steward came in to clean the cabin and he was horrified when he looked in the sink to see that

Rudi had pissed in it! Normally he couldn't speak a word of English but he managed to come out with, 'Washie, washie, not pissy, pissy' and stormed off!

The Mancini was fine for a while but Rudi and I never found it easy to stand still in business. We sold the Mancini for £35,000 and bought the 30-bedroomed St. George Hotel on Clifton Drive for £59,000. It was bigger and better with a beautiful lounge and a cabaret room and we felt as if we were really on our way. Mind you it wasn't all plain sailing and we got into trouble when we overbooked very badly at Christmas. We even had someone sleeping in our own bedroom because we couldn't turn anyone away at that time of the year. I was sleeping in the kitchen on a deckchair with Rudi's coat over me and he slept on top of the hot cupboard. The milkman walked into the kitchen in the morning and was so shocked he almost dropped his crate. But needs must in our business. You do whatever you have to do and the customers always have to come first.

But it was not long before the 70-bedroom Palm Court came on the market. Property prices were rising fast in 1978 and we sold the St. George for £135,000 and had to pay £250,000. The Palm Court had been struggling and that was part of the attraction for me. We looked at places that were busier but we thought there was so much less room for improvement. With the Palm Court we had the opportunity of really stamping our personalities on the place. Luxury of luxuries, it had a lift! We had more staff by then and I actually took on a chef for the first time instead of trying to do all the cooking myself. Both Rudi and I still seemed to be putting in as many hours as ever. But we enjoyed it, especially the way so many of the customers became our friends and followed us from place to place. And we still had plenty of laughs along the way.

We've had more than one death in our time and it is always very stressful. Once a lady in a big coach party from Manchester group passed away on their very last night with us. Her friend took me to one side after they had finished their dinner and said she thought she had died. She'd just finished her fish and chips, gone upstairs and died. I went up and she was sitting up in bed, dead as a doornail.

She said, 'Look, we've had a lovely time, it will really spoil things if everyone finds out now that she's died.' We'd called the ambulance by then and I found myself trying to pretend the poor woman was still alive but ill and I 'talked' to her as they brought her down the stairs. I was saying things like, 'I'm sure you'll feel better in the morning,' and 'You're going to the right place. It's a marvellous hospital.'

I thought I'd got away with it. But a sharp-eyed guest saw that the ambulance men both got into the front of the vehicle before they drove off and told everyone she must be dead!

That wasn't the only time I managed to talk myself into a difficult situation. I put a man and woman sleeping together and they weren't even married, or even a couple! We had seen them together the year before. They came back and she was in a room with her daughter. We thought this other chap was her husband and when the daughter left to do some exams, we thought we were being helpful by putting Mr Ellis's stuff in her room. Next morning I saw her and asked if she was all right. She said, 'Well, yes, but I am a bit tired. I've been up all night with that man you put in my room.' I said, 'You what?' She said I've been on the chair all night. There was a fella in my bed when I got back.' I was horrified. I said I thought it was her husband and asked her why she hadn't said something. She said, 'This is one of the first hotels I've stayed in and I've heard you have to share.' I said that's when you come with another woman, not with a strange man. Some people complain if there's a bit of litter on the floor, this woman said nothing even though there was a total stranger in her bed!

Rudi was right about my daughter Pamela. She did come back into my life. She used to come over to Blackpool to see me with my mum and we slowly rebuilt our relationship. She got pregnant when she was young and had to get married. I didn't go to the wedding but gradually we became closer. She used to come and see me and stay at the hotel. She had two daughters called Gemma and Adele. They were lovely girls but she had a bad marriage. I didn't like her husband and I hated his father after I discovered he was abusing his young granddaughters. Pamela went through hell with the girls being taken into care before it was proved the grandfather was responsible. It was a terribly upsetting time for everyone but eventually I helped her to get her daughters back. The kids were forced to go into court in their school uniforms. It was a terrible ordeal to put them through. There was a break in the court proceedings when a detective came to talk to me. He had video tapes in his hand containing interviews the girls had given. The grandfather was sitting nearby and he had still not admitted anything, which meant the girls had got to go into court. I knew he could hear me and I said loudly, 'What's those videos? Are they videos of my grandchildren being abused. Is that what I've got to watch?' We were not supposed to speak to him but I knew he could hear me and I knew I was intimidating him. I was wearing this bright orange coat and I was determined to be as threatening towards him as I could.

The police came to me shortly afterwards and said the grandfather was going to admit guilt. But after the court his wife was walking round arm in arm with this evil abusing man and I just lost my temper. His wife said she would stick by him and that enraged Pamela and I so much we attacked her and gave her a good battering. The police had to come out and stop it and she has never seen the grandchildren since. He had abused other kids in the area but she still went off with him. He was a vile monster and he's dead now, I'm delighted to say. It was a horrible experience, particularly for the little girls, but it did help to bring my daughter and I back to being very close again. She and my granddaughters live in Blackpool now and I see as much of them as I can. They each have a son and I am a very proud great-grandmother of Joshua and Michael.

It was while we were in the Palm Court that we had to ask one couple to move rooms and I was plunged into deep embarrassment when I came across all this sexual paraphernalia. This charming couple had been coming for ages. And they always liked the same room, number 53, on the front. It was one of the nicest rooms we had there. On this particular visit they had it for most of their stay but someone else had already booked it for the end of their time with us and they agreed to move out on the Sunday. On the day they were due to switch the chambermaid came to me in a panic: 'Mrs M, this couple have not come back and we've got people arriving to go in it.' Naturally, we never normally like to get involved with guests' possessions but this time we had no choice. There was no sign of them so I told the chambermaid that I knew them very well and I would help her move their things to the new room. She was only a young kid and we found all these sex toys and exotic underwear. The chambermaid was very embarrassed and I was a bit shocked myself. I think I must have been a bit out of touch with sexual appliances. Rudi and I always managed very happily making love with the equipment God gave us, although I knew all that sort of stuff was around.

When the couple came back they apologised profusely. They had forgotten they were supposed to be moving that morning and I explained that we had shifted all their stuff for them. To save their embarrassment, I laughed and said, 'I went up and did it myself. You've got one of those things that Rudi and I use, haven't you? They're great, aren't they?' She looked very relieved as she said, 'Oh do you use them? Yes they're wonderful.' You never stop learning about people in this business and I never make judgements.

We do get ridiculous complaints. The other day we had a guest whose mother comes here a lot and they were celebrating a birthday upstairs in the Tower Suite. He had come the night before and had a room above the Theatre Bar. We always warn anyone booked in there that music is played in the Theatre Bar until midnight and you can hear it. Most people say, 'Oh, we never go to bed before 12 o'clock anyway,' and don't mind. But if you take it, you have to accept there's noise in the evening. This fellow booked into the floor above, where we've never had any complaints from. But in the morning he came down and said, 'The baby wouldn't sleep last night because of the noise from the Theatre Bar. We should have been told.' I overheard the conversation and was concerned. I said I was sorry and he moaned on that he had come for his mother's birthday. I said, 'Would you like to move rooms?' 'No,' he said, 'we're fine where we are. We're going to the party tonight and we'll be up late so it doesn't matter.' I said, 'Fine,' and I asked one of my staff to give them a bottle of wine to say sorry. As I was walking away I overheard him say, 'A bottle of wine's not going to do this.' I was shocked by his attitude and I left it to my manager to deal with. He didn't give them a penny back so that guy talked himself out of a bottle of wine.

Most of our guests are thoroughly decent members of the public. They're as straight as a die and they just want a hotel that gives them a fair deal for their money and that's what we always strive to do. But there are bad people out there as well. There is one woman I know about who goes on holiday and deliberately does things in hotels to get herself free meals or holidays. She has a string of tricks like putting hairs on her food or making a mess in her room that she uses to make a false claim on the hotel. She does it all the time and generally she gets away with it. Years ago I was on a boat bound for the Canaries and there was this group of women who claimed to have all sorts of things stolen that they had never had in the first place. It's very hard to disprove and they often get compensation that they have no right to.

But one part of me is not acting - I genuinely like people. I don't care what creed or colour they are. I enjoy dealing with them because I'm in the entertainment business and if I can make their stay with me even a tiny bit happier by sharing a laugh in the lift or the lounge then I feel as if I'm doing my job. I'm interested in people and their lives. We get all sorts of folk in Blackpool and I'm always curious to know what brings them here and their memories and hopes for the future.

You have to develop all kinds of tricks of the trade to deal with awkward customers. Once I had to pretend to sack the receptionist because she had overbooked and we had no room for a particularly demanding regular customer. We were completely full and Mrs Jackson arrived fully expecting to be escorted to her usual room. I wondered how we were going to get out of this. The lady in question was getting on a bit to an age when they like to know exactly where their room is. I said to the chambermaid, 'Just stand there and take whatever grief I give you'. So I said, 'I'm very sorry Mrs Jackson, this girl had made a terrible mistake and overbooked, I'm afraid I'm going to have to put you into the hotel next door.' Mrs Jackson's temperature visibly rose by several degrees but I ignored her and continued, 'As a result, this girl has been dismissed.' Mrs Jackson's attitude changed instantly. She said, 'Oh please, don't sack her on my account. I couldn't bear it. That would be awful. I will be quite comfortable next door, I'm sure,' and the potential problem disappeared. She only had to spend two nights next door before we brought her back to her favourite room.

Another time a guy rang up and said, 'I am coming with a party but I need to have a double room to myself'. And then a bit later, unknown to me, he cancelled it. Then he 'phoned me back and said, 'I had to cancel it because my wife was standing next to me.' She must have found out he'd booked a double room, and he then said he did want the double after all. I agreed and even Chief Inspector Barnaby could have worked out that he wasn't planning to spend the night reading a book. But his wife was evidently suspicious and she turned up at the hotel that night at about six o'clock. She found out his room number and went up and discovered him with another woman and just about screamed the place down. Somehow we got her out of there, but it wasn't easy. Her husband went after her and the other poor woman was left in the room on her own.

We began in the days when unmarried couples used to sign in as Mr and Mrs Smith. I had been through all that with Rudi myself so I was never too bothered whether guests who were sharing a room were married to each other, or as often happened, to other people. But you could just tell from the nervousness of the couple when they arrived whether or not they were really married.

Girls are much worse for sneaking men into their rooms than the other way round. One night we had a couple of girls who both had blokes with them and it was pretty obvious they were becoming more than a little friendly in the bar. I said to my husband, 'They're not going to go home tonight, they are getting much too close.' The guys left and the girls went up to their rooms. I left it for a while and then went and got the master key. I opened the door and there was this lad in bed with one of the girls. I pulled the sheet off him and told him to get out. It wasn't a question of morality, it was just business. We never care if somebody wants to sleep with someone else but if they want to stay in our hotel we felt they should pay us. He hadn't paid, so he wasn't staying. And he hadn't got a stitch on. He was most indignant and said, 'I'm a soldier in Northern Ireland.' I said, 'Well I don't think much of your weapon. Get out.'

We didn't give keys out in the earlier days. They had to ring if they were late back and we would get up and let them in. There was a woman guest who had once got away with sneaking somebody up to her room and she was out late again. She didn't come back until half past four with a feller. I think she thought we just wouldn't notice him at that time of night. But we sat waiting for her and stopped him.

That was over 20 years ago. It's always gone on. Nowadays we have night porters on and we know who's who and what's what. If people overstay their welcome in the bar, the bar staff check their room keys.

People like to let their hair down in Blackpool. They will do things here that they would never do at home. There's always been a buzz about the place and I hope there always will be. In the old days it was just dead exciting. There was none of this baring your bottom in the street and binge drinking and getting absolutely paralytic and fighting. Years ago there was an innocence about the place. Men and women went on donkey rides on the beach. That wouldn't be allowed today. As a teenager I once got so excited with all the jogging up and down on a donkey that I was laughing so much I peed myself. I was here with all my friends and we had a wonderful time. It was an escape from the rat race where you lived at home. We all lived in terraced houses and the muck from the great mills, factories and the pits. It was magic to come here to the lovely beach and all this open space. Manchester in those days was often covered in a sort of hazy industrial fog and we had smog masks during the winter, but when you came up to Blackpool the air was clear and fresh and somehow the sun always seemed to be shining.

Human nature is my favourite subject. In my job you have to deal with it all the time. But you learn that as you go along. I had no idea when I started in this business that I would be able to handle people. It's a bit like being an actress as well because you have to be different things to different people. Every night now at the Queens I take great care in getting ready for dinner and going down and talking to guests. For me it's like being in show business. You might have a big fat tax bill waiting upstairs but downstairs you have to have look as if you haven't got a care in the world with a big smile on your face and a real interest in all your guests.

It was in 1979 that we were able to afford our first stay in a five star hotel, the Reina Isabel in Las Palmas. We had been to Gran Canaria before and stayed in an apartment above a pub. We had a good time but we used to walk past this beautiful hotel and think, 'One day we will be able to stay there'. When we could finally afford it we went for a month and it was an amazing experience. I will always remember a young Indian boy there who could speak Indian, English and Spanish perfectly but, in spite of being very clever, he had obviously had such a privileged upbringing there were certain aching gaps in his education. One morning without his parents at breakfast, he was presented with a boiled egg. He was completely bewildered and had to call the head waiter over to enquire how to deal with it. Rudi and I couldn't believe it. This kid could speak three languages but he couldn't open a boiled egg! But the hotel was fabulous and one of my nieces is called Reina, Queen in Spanish, after that wonderful hotel.

We were in the Palm Court for six very successful years. My sister Sharron came to work for me on reception because her husband was working abroad. Rudi's son Raymond was a regular visitor at that time. He was married with three children by then. I like to think I always keep my eye on what's going on in the hotel but neither Rudi nor I had any idea that a romance was building between Sharron and Raymond. It was a love that lasted as they have now been married for 27 years and have three lovely children, Victoria, Claudia and Reina (after the hotel). Running away with married women must be in the Mancini family. Rudi's father ran away from Italy with a married woman. Rudi ran away with me. And Raymond ran away with Sharron. Incidentally this means that Raymond and Sharron's daughters are my step-grandchildren as well as my nieces as Raymond is my brother in law as well as my stepson!

When the Queens Hotel, an establishment that meant so much to both of us, came on the market in 1985 we had to go for it. They wanted £700,000 for the place where I had first worked in Blackpool as a very much in love runaway lover for £8.50 a week. We managed to get £400,000 for the Palm Court and with the help of a mortgage that has mercifully long since been paid off we bought the Queens Hotel. Today I'm still here as proud boss of the largest independently owned hotel in Blackpool. We only made it by the skin of our teeth. Bankers told me to steer clear. The roof was hanging off as the building had been sadly let go and it was in a terrible state. We knew it needed lots of money spending on in but we could see the potential. The Queens Hotel has real history.

It is where countless guests have enjoyed the best resort in Britain and we knew if we worked as hard as ever we could attract enough of them back to make a success of the place. When I walked back in here I did not feel apprehensive as I so often did. Instead I felt instantly at home. We wanted it and we got it and I still love it. It has a wonderful history and today it is just run as a friendly family hotel. I'm very proud of it. We have 110 bedrooms here and every one of them could tell a story.

I always ask people about the food. I used to go round after dinner getting the verdict on our meals straight from the customers' mouths. Do they like it and are they getting enough? Recently a lady guest said that the portions were not large enough. She and her family could have eaten more food. I went and played hell with the staff in the kitchens.

You have to be tough in this business. I remember about ten years ago I woke in the middle of the night. I couldn't sleep so I went downstairs for a cup of tea. At four o'clock in the morning I found every light on and all the tables uncleared. The night porter was asleep in a chair clutching an empty bottle of strong lager. When I woke him he was full of apologies. He was sure I was going to sack him on the spot. But I just told him to clear up, wash up and set all the tables for breakfast. He only just made it and then I told him, 'Now you're sacked!'

It has changed so much over the years. In our early days we were catering for people who lived in a pretty basic two-up, two-down terraced house with no central heating and the toilet down the yard, just like the one I was brought up in, so even a small boarding house seemed glamorous to them. Even if there were 14 bedrooms and only four toilets it still seemed like a step up in the world. In some places we had family rooms with up to eight people sharing one sink and no-one ever complained. But there has been a drastic improvement in people's living conditions. At home they have their bathrooms en suite and their central heating and all the mod cons of today so even though hotels have raised their standards enormously it is hard to provide the same sort of contrast.

After we bought the Queens, Rudi and I decided that, instead of living in the hotel, it was time we had a home of our own and we bought a house. It was a lovely place in Lytham and it cost a fortune. The business was doing really well. We had earned a lot of money and we thought we might as well spend it. The curtains alone cost £35,000. Every bedroom had its own bathroom. We had a wonderful marble suite. No expense was spared, and it was absolutely magnificent. We even had a brand new grand piano. Everything was perfect. But on our first night there Rudi and I both realised it just did not feel right. We only slept in it one night and then we went back to our flat in the Queens. We just couldn't do it. This was in 1987 and after always living together in flats and hotels we just felt uncomfortable in this big house. We sold it later and never regretted it.

Rudi never played the organ here in the Queens, apart from occasional private parties. He used to say he was frightened of not being able to read the music because his eyesight was deteriorating with age. 'It looks like fly shit to me', he used to say. He was an exceptional musician and when we bought this place he was 65 and he felt he wanted to stop when he was still performing well. He used to say to me that he was frightened of not being able to 'find the bloody note'. But privately he always played. He loved his music and he practised every day until the day he died.

We were both very happy with that decision because as the hotel became more successful we were able to catch up on lost time with all the things we had put off doing for years because we'd been so busy. We learned a lot along the way about each other, Rudi and I. We enjoyed staying in that simple hotel in Majorca when we first started in the boarding house trade but gradually, as we went on, we have been able to afford to stay at places with a few stars next to their name. We educated ourselves in the finer things of life as we became able to afford it. We gave each other confidence as we grew together. We stayed at the Dorchester and we flew on Concorde.

I never set out to be rich. It just sort of happened. As I got into the boarding house business I saw how money could come in if you did a good job and made a decent business. Then I did become a bit avaricious and started trying hard to make money. It was Rudi's business training and my energy I suppose. He taught me. As he got older and I became more experienced I gradually took over from him as the driving force I suppose. He told me to run it how I wanted to. There are lots of people who have run boarding houses in Blackpool who have never made a bean. But in the 1960s it was a great business to be in. There were so many people coming here looking for somewhere to stay you could let a toilet. In fact when you think of some of the dodgy accommodation, some people did exactly that. We had even let the swing-seat outside in the back garden in St. Bede's Avenue! Blackpool was the number one holiday destination in Europe. There's a wonderful warmth in the town that I've never experienced anywhere else in the world. It's still top although we only get around nine million visitors compared to 17 million years ago. And the constant rise in the price of property helped us as well because every time we traded up to a bigger and better place we made money. Sadly those days have gone, perhaps for ever.

9

Rudi

Rudi loved the Queens Hotel. He was never happier than when he was downstairs chatting happily to our guests. I did the main running of the place and I was always making an excuse to get away because I had some jobs to do. Rudi never found it so easy to break away from people and he would sometimes sit there until the early hours of the morning. He was always concerned that guests would think he was ignorant if he went off to bed early.

The Queens was always very special to Rudi although his first experience with the place was not too happy. It was during the war, when on leave from the RAF, Rudi visited Blackpool. He always had long hair and he passed in front of the Queens, which had been commandeered for the duration of the war by the Air Force. An officer saw Rudi in his uniform out on the front and shouted 'Come here airman. Your hair is too long. Get it cut'. He had to leave the girl he had met and be brought in to get his haircut here in the Queens by an RAF barber. He never found the girl again.

Rudi had joined up at the start of the war and he took his accordion with him. He was always worried about his hands because they were so vital to him as a musician. He was not best pleased when one of his first postings was to Benbecula in the Outer Hebrides. They used to go round to all the crofters' homes every week to invite as many local girls as possible to the dance on a Saturday night. They had great dances and

Rudi would play and play and play all night and they would leave whisky for him on the piano. He told me that one night he got very drunk on whisky and felt so awful the next day he never, ever touched whisky again. Years later we went to see the place for old times sake and when we landed there it was like landing on the bloody moon.

One week he was asked to play in the Officers' Mess where they had a few dos of their own. Rudi got fed up with this and thought that everyone who joined up got put in with people from the same trade. The engineers were all together so why shouldn't he be in with the musicians, he thought. He complained that he was being made to play for them after working all day peeling potatoes in the freezing cold, which was playing havoc with his delicate and crucially important fingers. 'My hands have to be flexible to do what I do. I should be a musician,' he would say. Anyway, one night they had him playing and the next day he was peeling the spuds and cleaning out the latrines and at night he was put on guard. As he explained to me, being on guard in the Outer Hebrides was ridiculous. There was no-one else around for miles and it was dead quiet. You couldn't even hear a dog barking. He thought, 'Fuck this' and went to bed. He woke up to find guns pointing at his head. 'Mancini, get up,' the enraged officer ordered. ' You could be shot for this. You deserted your post.' Rudi replied: 'Sir you can shoot me if you like, but there is no way I am peeling potatoes in the morning, cleaning toilets for you in the afternoon, playing music for you at night and then going on guard duty. I've had enough.' He was thrown in the guardhouse. But there was another officer there who was a member of the W.H.Smith family from Manchester and he had a word with Rudi and said he would sort something out. A few weeks later he was told, 'Mancini, there is someone to see you.' It was a scout from the Ralph Reader Gang Show who said a Mr Smith had been in touch and he was here to conduct an audition. He just said, 'Play something'.

Rudi thought this was his chance. He decided to play *Flight of the Bumble Bee*, a difficult piece which requires very good musical technique and he just started to play. He got through eight bars when the scout told him to stop. Rudi thought he had blown his big chance but the scout said, 'Mancini, I will be back in two days for you'. He was from the Ralph Reader Gang Show and from that day until the end of the War, Rudi was a musician not a airman, and he had a wonderful time. He toured the world and every so often would come back to London to rehearse. And that is when he met and played for people like Peter Sellers, Cardew Robinson and Dick Emery who were comparatively unknown at the time but who became household names after the war.

He never had to shoot a gun in anger but did entertain troops all over the world, often performing on the back of a lorry just behind the front line so it was a life that included danger as well as glamour and excitement. Rudi loved it.

Once Rudi was somewhere in France with Cardew the Cad as they called him, when they got a little too near the action. The army was engaged in bitter hand-to-hand fighting with the Germans and as soon as they arrived the Gang Show was asked what weapons they could lay their hands on. 'Well, I've got a penknife,' said Cardew brightly, but fortunately he was not required to use it in anger. Rudi was always impressed by Cardew's ability to attract women. He was tall and gawky and cheerfully admitted, 'I'm no oil painting, in fact I'm not even a water colour'. But he got all the girls he could handle and Rudi was forever a fan. He was wonderful with his patter. I got him to come up to help one of my charitable functions and although he was getting on in life then, his speech was absolutely hilarious. He had the whole audience in fits of laughter and we made so much for a good cause that day because he had them eating out of his hand.

They also went to Hawaii and entertained American forces and eventually they had flown just about all over the world as a huge morale booster for the Allied troops. They did some marvellous shows in great cities and wonderful concert halls as well as on improvised lorries or whatever. It was a very exciting time for Rudi. His face used to light up when he told the stories of his war. He just loved to entertain people and if it was helping the war effort as well then he was doubly delighted.

At the end of the war, Ralph Reader asked Rudi along with lots of the others to sign contracts to keep on entertaining but Rudi wouldn't. The majority of the acts and musicians stayed on but Rudi wouldn't because he knew most of the work would be in London and he wanted to come straight back up North to Manchester. Always very aware of his strong northern accent, he felt a little uncomfortable with mostly well-spoken southerners and decided to come home. He was king in Manchester. He was the only one playing great music live at that time and the big Italian community all loved him so he had a ready made audience waiting to welcome him home. He once said to me, 'In London I was just nobody, but in Manchester I am Rudi Mancini and he is somebody'. But whenever we went to reunions or when Cardew came to visit, they would always talk about the old days and while some had done well and others had fallen by the wayside, Rudi never worried about what might have been. He was always happy with his decision to come home.

I never expected we would get to a silver wedding because we had both been married before. But we reached our 25th wedding anniversary in April 1998 and went to Paris to celebrate. And when we got out of the limo outside the Ritz in front of those famous doors we said to each other, 'How the bleeding hell did we get here?' We always said that would be the title of our book.

Rudi had always had troubles with indigestion. He first became ill with pancreatitis back in 1973 and he was taken into hospital. The doctors kept asking him if he was a big drinker and he said no because he only ever had the occasional social gin and tonic. I was doubly busy then without him and that was when I resolved to learn to drive. I was lost without Rudi in more ways than one. He came out of hospital, but after we were installed in the Queens he thought he needed an operation for a hiatus hernia. We were fortunate really because a friend of ours, Carol Allcott, who was chief matron at the BUPA Fylde Coast Hospital in Blackpool, quickly got him an appointment. Later she phoned me to come in and see Rudi. They had found an ulcer so the operation was to be postponed. When I got back I knew something was wrong because everyone was round the bed. The bad news was that Rudi had a cancer on his oesophagus. They were going to operate to remove it. I thought it was a death sentence. Next day the sight of him in intensive care was absolutely horrendous. On the side of the breathing machine he was attached to it said Supplied by the Queendeans Charity. He pulled through after that first big scare in 1986 and that helped inspire me to work harder and harder to raise more money for charity. But if Carol Allcott hadn't got him straight in to hospital he would have put it off, I know he would.

Rudi died in 1998. He was just 78 years old and I've missed him every minute of every day since. He died here and it was horrendous. I was so devastated I lost a stone in a week.

I've never wanted to move on. I tried to give him a funeral fit for a king. We had 13 black limousines, the hearse and another car for the flowers plus lots of people following us. The first service was at the Sacred Heart in Blackpool because I wanted his friends to be able to come. Gina Brannelli sang Italian songs and played the accordion. We all got in the cars after the service and drove down the Promenade. The whole fleet stopped outside the Queens and the staff stood with the Union Jack and the Italian flag and a policeman with his hat in his hands. Then we went down the motorway to Manchester. But because we'd been up so early we needed a wee, so the limos stopped at the motorway services. It was quite a sight. We eventually got to Ancoats in Manchester and saw more crowds gathering in St Michael's. The church was full. All the Italians came out as we had another mass and Gina and the priest came with us. The Italian songs went down well and we needed police to look after the crowds. At the cemetery

I saw Chubby Brown, and Jeremy Beadle. Afterwards we all went back to the Midland Hotel in Manchester and I found myself looking out for where Rudi would be sitting as I always did. Then I realised I'd never do that job again; it was very sad. Jeremy came back to see me, and not for the first time, he made me laugh. He was clearly upset and he said, 'I was in that graveyard and someone came up and asked for an autograph'. Jeremy is always very polite to the public but he admitted he just lost his temper for a moment and said, 'Fuck off, I'm not here for that.' Rudi wanted to be buried in Manchester near all his Italian friends and Jeremy wanted to mourn his friend without the burden of celebrity for once.

10

The Show Must Go On

The Queens Hotel had become our happiest home. And we were helped to keep it that way by some of the many entertainers who have visited the place over the years and become good friends. It's a long list of special entertainment pals that includes, in no particular order, Les Dawson, Garry Bushell, Derek Batey, Russell Watson, Danny la Rue, Chubby Brown, Bernard Manning, Esther Rantzen, Lenny Henry, Vernon Kaye, Roy Walker and Norman Collier.

Rudi had died in November and really over Christmas and New Year I was out of it. I just couldn't get my head round it. After everything we had been through together our love was stronger than ever and I was just devastated. I didn't want to do anything. I didn't want to work. I didn't want to go downstairs to meet the guests but at the same time I didn't want to stay up in my flat in the hotel on my own. I didn't drink. Drink to me has always been a social thing, a happy thing. I knew alcohol would not drown my sorrows, it would make them feel even worse. I just sat alone in my flat in the hotel with its view of the Irish Sea. Weight fell off me. I went to London on my own and then made myself feel even worse by going to places where we had gone together. I made myself feel a lot worse by walking around London crying. It was a terrible time. I'm pretty tough and I know I can handle most things in life but for once I was completely floored. I had lived with the man I loved for over 30 years and the truth is that I didn't just love him, I absolutely worshipped him.

Then one night Johnny Casson, who was appearing on the pier, came in with Ann Marie and his friend Joe Longthorne and his partner Jamie Moran and they persuaded me to go downstairs and have a chat with them. I was all in black and still desperately down. I'd never met Joe before but I'd enjoyed his show very much and I thought, being in show business, he might like champagne. He looked at me and he said I reminded him of his sister. We got chatting and it was like the endless feeling of grief was lifted off me. I can't describe the feeling exactly because it was a bit unreal. My emotions were all over the place at the time but something in Joe's personality rang a bell with me. Something happened that I can't really explain. We just talked and gradually I felt a little bit easier about myself for the first time in months. After he went I felt quite different.

As I walked back up the corridor to my flat in the hotel I started to sing for the first time since Rudi had died. I sang *I Wanna Be Where You Are*. It's one of my favourite songs and later Rudi's daughter Angela heard it in the background when she was on the 'phone and she was quite alarmed. 'You're not playing that for my Dad, are you? You're not going to do anything stupid are you?' It wasn't that at all. I realised I didn't want to be at home for Rudi's birthday or mine. I said to my sister, 'I don't want to be here. Let's go to Las Vegas!' I had been with Rudi a couple of times and I knew Vegas would be so hectic I wouldn't have time to sit and be sad. My sister's suitcase went missing on the way to the hotel but we weren't that bothered. I said she could borrow some of my stuff. But on the evening of our first day there was a big bang on the door and there was this fellow with her case. She was delighted but I was transfixed by the name on his badge. He was called Rudi! It was my birthday and I was just so moved I gave him a big tip. Back in Blackpool I heard from the hotel that Joe Longthorne was staying which somehow cheered me, even though we had only had that one meeting.

After I got back I saw a bit more of Joe and realised what a wonderful guy he is. He's had his problems certainly, but he has overcome them and he has become a great friend to me. A little later he told me he was doing a tour of Australia and asked me to come with him. I was astonished. I thought, 'That's such a long way!' He said, 'We have a week in Thailand, first,' and talked me into coming with him for two of the six week tour. I met him and his band at Heathrow Airport. It was just like an adventure. We had a week at the fabulous hotel and then we went on the tour. From the moment I met Joe and Jamie at the airport I had a wonderful time and stayed for all six weeks. It was very exciting. I couldn't believe it was happening to me. In Sydney we climbed to the top Harbour Bridge at night. When I got to the top I was sorry there was no shop or café where you could buy a nice cup of tea. I even did a radio phone-in with Jeremy Beadle on Radio London. And most embarrassingly I got an earring stuck up Joe Longthorne's nose one night when the music was so loud he was trying to hear what I was saying!

It was friends like Joe who helped me get through the awful time after Rudi's death. Other great friends like Mick Miller and Roy 'Chubby' Brown helped me as well in different ways. Chubby even worked at the Queens when he was a kid and Mick is also a very close pal. I've known them for years and they were really there for me when I needed them.

Running a hotel feels a little like being in showbusiness at times and we had a talent competition in the early days at the Queens Hotel. Every Thursday we used to assemble the most extraordinary characters. It became quite well known. We used to go to the Gang Show reunions nearly every year when there were still enough of them alive. Then I got a call to say that someone from Channel 4, a television producer called Mark Chapman, was coming to look at our talent show as they were looking for ideas for programmes. He was interested in artists who had been on the boards years ago but who had become largely forgotten. They called it *Old Faces*. Mark was a marvellously enthusiastic producer and insisted on making his programme on film. Eventually it got on Channel 4 but they put it out on New Year's Eve and it pretty well got lost with all the celebrations going on that night. Mark Chapman has gone on to much greater things but the love and care he put into that show was remarkable.

Months later I turned on the television at my sister's to watch Michael Barrymore's *My Kind Of People* show and saw that the first two people they had on were two that had been on our little show in the Theatre Bar. He went for characters and I think the idea came from our little show. We had some wonderful old acts. Who could forget the Rumbergers? Weeks after that I got a telephone call from the *Barrymore Show* asking me and Rudi to appear with Barrymore and introduce some of our acts. Neville sang *Say It With Flowers*. He got a letter from Dorothy Squires to say how wonderfully she thought he had put her song over.

That appearance led to one of my great friendships of later life - with Jeremy Beadle no less! I was so enthused by that TV appearance that I wrote in to Jeremy Beadle's wonderful programme *Beadle's About* and suggested he play a trick on a girl I knew. Carol was larger than life and she had a fantastic, hearty laugh. She was a very jolly person. I sent him some photos and finished up helping to set up the joke. I helped to persuade her to look after a big shop opening in Blackpool for a friend. I laid it on a bit and told her it had to be all very hush-hush. With Jeremy Beadle's people I set it all up and I did not even tell Rudi because he could never keep a secret. I did not tell Rudi until we had got in the cab on the way to the Hilton for the screening. It was a balloon shop and Carol was told she had to take care of the place until the mayor arrived. I was recruited as one of the mayor's party in the hope that would convince her it was genuine. Carol had been briefed that it was desperately important that this shop was a success. And she had to sing *Up, Up and Away in My Beautiful Balloon* when the mayor arrived. We could hear all this listening on the TV bus going to spring the joke on the poor girl. Jeremy Beadle was on the bus, dressed in a boiler suit getting ready to pull off his big surprise. The balloons started popping and Carol frantically tried to cope and when the mayor arrived she did a big curtsey. When the balloons started banging we had to pretend that we thought they had been sabotaged by this other company. They pretended they thought it was gunshots and called the police and Carol would not let the police in because she had been told to keep everyone out until we arrived. Jeremy finally did the big reveal and it all went very well. It was the start of a wonderful friendship because I found Jeremy was a tremendous person.

When he was in Blackpool he wanted to go and see as many shows as he could because he just loved live entertainment. At night-time he had waited for Frank Carson and Norman Collier and came back to our bar and sat talking with Rudi and I. We'd had a great day. Jeremy wanted me to show him the Theatre Bar, which was packed at the time, and he insisted on taking me right into the middle of the dance floor and dancing with me. The punters couldn't believe what was going on. He couldn't dance to save his life but he swung me round with great enthusiasm. Later I asked him why he'd done it. He explained that I had helped set up one of his comedy routines and this was his way of paying me back. He said, 'You've helped me with my business and I wanted to do something to help with yours. Jeremy Beadle going in the bar ought to be a bit of a talking point for a while!' He was very kind and thoughtful, a great guy. On the way back from a panto in Liverpool he stopped his limo in this decidedly dodgy area and insisted we all went into this rough pub for a drink. I said, 'Oh, Jeremy, this is not a good place'. But he had such confidence and love of life there was no stopping him. He said, 'Let's get in.' It was grim. Our feet stuck to the floor. There was a man behind the bar with two teeth, who looked about 83. There was a woman covered in tattoos playing darts on her own. Jeremy just brought the place alive. He bought a few drinks, had a game of darts and charmed everyone in the pub. They recognised him straight away of course and they loved the way he had no side to him. He knew he had brought a little sunshine into a few grey lives and he was delighted. He told me, 'These are the people who have given me a living.' He had no time for pomposity and self-importance and would just as soon chat with a roadsweeper as some jumped-up businessman. Of course he soon had the punters eating out of his hand. He genuinely loved people. Shortly before he died he asked me to go with him and some other friends on a working holiday to Turkey. I went with Jeremy and his wife Sue, his producer Mark Simpson and two friends, Loretta and Maurice. Mark has become one of my dearest friends and we holiday together and he visits me in Blackpool as often as he can. The Turkish holiday was wonderful and we had a great time. Jeremy was a smashing man.

It was Jeremy who first called me The Queen of Blackpool. Whenever he came up to Blackpool or I went down to London to one of his big dos he would introduce other people, including other famous names like Chris Tarrant or whoever, and leave me right to the end and then give me this big build up and say, 'And now, my friend, Pat Mancini, the Queen of Blackpool'. He would push me to the front and at first I felt like crawling under the table but gradually I got to enjoy and appreciate the attention.

Fame itself doesn't impress me and lots of my closest friends are anything but well known. But it just so happens that I've come into contact with some household names and many of them are wonderful people as well. Jeremy was a real man of the people who died much too young. He just loved people. At his funeral everyone had a tale to tell about him helping them along the way. It didn't matter to Jeremy whether or not you were famous.

I have gone back to Manchester many times over the years, but the funniest visit I made was for a school reunion. I took the Rolls and arranged to meet Frank 'Foo Foo' Lamarr in the Piccadilly Hotel. 'I'll be heavily veiled, darling,' said Frank with typical style. We were ensconced in this posh hotel when two quite rough looking girls came in, looking very out of place even though they'd made a bit of an effort. I said, 'At least they've tried,' and Frank deadpanned back wonderfully, 'Darling, you can't polish a turd.'

11

Charity

Until I came to the Queens I never had time to even think about working for charity. I was too busy working hard to make enough money to keep the business alive. But at the Queens it was different. All those years of scrimping and saving for the first time in my life, I had to admit I couldn't do everything myself. Rudi and I needed help and we set about hiring staff. I like to think I'm not a bad judge of people and I'm happy to say that most of the workers we took on at the Queens were loyal and very hard-working. The old place was in a terrible state when we took over - otherwise we'd never have been able to afford it! But gradually, and with a lot of loving care, we revived the lovely building and tried to restore some of its former glory.

When I first arrived at the Queens I soon realised that some of the staff were sadly not up to expectations. I was determined to build a top class team and swiftly advertised for new staff. Alice Pisacane applied for a job as a receptionist and two weeks after she was appointed I could see her potential and promoted her to be head receptionist. It is one of the best decisions I've ever made and she is still with me today some 23 years later. About a month later we were looking for a new manager and Alice asked me if her husband could apply. Initially I was against employing both members of a married couple but Joe Pisacane was such an outstanding candidate that he got the job. Rudi was particularly impressed that Joe could make spaghetti. He's still there today as well. We have a great and loyal team which also includes Jack Torrance, an ex-skater from the Pleasure Beach who is restaurant manager, Janet Duckworth and Alan Sergeant in accounts, Alex Hallett our duty manager, Irene Holborn and John Bolton who run the bars, and housekeeper Denise Fry. And our long serving chef Peter Crozier retired recently after 21 years with us. They're a great team and they help to make the Queens Hotel a success.

Once the show was properly on the road I found myself with a new and priceless luxury - time. That was when I began to become very much involved with charity work. I still controlled the hotel and remained very involved with the day to day running of the business but I was able to delegate so much of the work I actually had some spare energy. It felt marvellous because I knew exactly how to use it. Blackpool has been very good to me so I felt it was right that I should give something back.

Already installed at the Queens was a registered charity called the Queendeans Association. It was started before the war by a man called Dean and its headquarters were in our hotel. Originally it was a men-only affair which conducted its affairs in the smoke room. I got rid of the smoke room when I arrived, because I didn't like the sound of it. After we had bought the Queens, the previous owner Les Firth said he had forgotten to mention the Queendeans who had a little rent-free office upstairs. I was keen to keep supporting such a good cause but there was a problem - I was a woman! This all-male organisation was not initially very keen on having me as a member. But I suggested I form an all female committee to be called the Queenbees. They weren't too keen on a feminine rival so they instantly changed their rules and invited me on board. So I got involved and I've really enjoyed myself working for good causes. I've done all sorts for them. I've spent nights inside prison for them. I've done lap-dancing and pole-dancing for them! I went to prison with my friend Tracy Dawson, widow of the wonderful comedian Les Dawson, and I did the pole-dancing with another pal, Maxine Barry, who incidentally does a fabulous impression of Shirley Bassey. I've collected late at night with a charity bucket on the end of the pier for them. We've had all sorts of functions.

Once people hear you're a keen charity supporter you receive requests to help out all sorts of other charities. I've done a lot for the blind and finished up as executive president of the Blackpool Society for the Blind and president of the Polio Association. In my life I've seen plenty of people in desperate times, people who have so little, and it is such a joy to be able to help them out. The Queendeans have helped so many different sections of the community, for the deaf, the blind, the limbless, physically and mentally handicapped children, hospitals, hospices, girl guides, boy scouts, churches, schools, pensioners - anyone who needs a bit of a helping hand in life. They don't hand over money, they only give goods and over the years I'm delighted to say we've helped many, many needy people.

I was very proud to hear, at the end of 2006, that I was to receive the MBE in the New Year's Honours List for my charity work. It represented a wonderful thank-you for 20 years of rattling tins and consciences. I think I've helped to raise more than £2 million. I was absolutely overwhelmed to receive such an honour. I just wished my mum and Rudi could have still been around to share it with. When I got the letter I cried and cried and I did the obvious thing and went to visit their graves.

It was a magical day when I went to Buckingham Palace to receive my MBE from Prince Charles. I can remember every detail but it all seemed to flash past in a dream. I took my brother Paul and my sister Sharron and daughter Pamela with me and it was a day we will never forget. I told Prince Charles all about going to prison for the night for charity. I did it with Les Dawson's widow Tracey and we raised £7,000 for charity. Prince Charles seemed very caring and interested. He was a real Prince Charming. Our trip to London was made complete when we were invited to have lunch at the House of Commons by Nigel Evans MP. It was simply the icing on the cake.

Not all my visits to London are quite so upmarket. Gay pal Peter Watson, who runs Anton's café bar in St Anne's with his partner Paul Lomax, is one of my favourite companions and we usually find ourselves having a laugh. We certainly did the time we were in Harrods. I was in a changing room at the Armani department trying on a suit, with Peter outside guarding my most recent purchases, when a voice on the Tannoy announced that singing star Englebert Humperdinck was in the sound and vision department signing autographs. I panicked because I knew Englebert was one of Peter's idols. I dashed outside in my bra and pants and screamed at Peter, 'Don't you dare move.' I needed a throwaway camera very quickly and after a snooty Harrods employee directed me to Boots for such a downmarket item I dashed back to capture Peter's moment with Englebert. The singer himself was charming to both of us, a real gentleman. I'm pleased he didn't see me yelling in my bra and pants!

Peter and I certainly have our moments. Another time we were in London to watch the *X Factor* finals, we finished up in the Shadow Lounge in Soho, a top gay nightspot. I always feel safe and cared for in gay company but when I went outside to get a taxi I didn't feel too safe when a man came from nowhere and put his hand in my bag and tried to grab some of the cash inside. Without thinking I smacked him round the face and knocked him flying and the bouncers came and helped me deal with him. To make matters worse it was pouring with rain and we couldn't get a taxi to our apartment. We finished up getting a ride in a bicycle-drawn rickshaw which was a huge laugh, until we got pulled up by the police! I thought I'd hit the thief so hard I'd hurt or even killed him and I was really worried. But it turned out that the lights on the back of the rickshaw were not working. We had to get out and walk the rest of the way!

It's a completely new phase of my life now, without Rudi. And I have to do lots of things I'd never have dared attempt in the past. I've always hated flying but when Frank Carson invited me to come and watch him work in Dubai I conquered my fear and climbed on board. I even took a flight on my own to see some other friends in Malta on the way home. Rudi would be very proud of me!

Now as I sit writing the story of my life in my beloved old Queens Hotel I realise just how much I love the place. I did try to move out and live a normal life once but it didn't work. We bought a lovely house down the coast but I only stayed in it for one night. I couldn't stand it. I was too lonely.

This old place has been home to me for such a long time I'm reluctant to leave but I can't stay here forever. I've got plenty of happy memories to keep me company but I've got a few sad ones as well. Dean's death is something I'll never ever really get over and Rudi's passing was so very tragic as well. I know I'm lucky to have met a man I really loved so deeply but I'm still sorry that our love hurt so many other people. I always regretted being away from Blackpool when my mother died. I went to America, just for six days, and perhaps because of some strange premonition, I gave her a kiss for just about the first time just before I left. Tragically she died the day I came home.

Even today I love to be involved. Financially I've no need to set foot in the place but that's not my way. I like the people and I like to meet them and have a chat. So many of them have become good friends over the years. And the Queens Hotel is one of my friends as well. If I see anything out of place I put it straight. They call me the Queen of Blackpool and it's very kind of them but I can't reign forever. Who knows how long I'll last? But it's been a wonderful journey - thanks for joining me along the way.